SPIRITUAL DIARY

An Inspirational Thought
for Each Day

*Chiefly Selections from
the Writings of*

PARAMAHANSA YOGANANDA

Published by
SELF-REALIZATION FELLOWSHIP
3880 San Rafael Avenue
Los Angeles, California

1977

Spiritual Diary

 Authorized by the International Publications
Council of Self-Realization Fellowship

Self-Realization Fellowship
3880 San Rafael Avenue
Los Angeles, California 90065, U.S.A.

2227–877–25M
ISBN: 0–87612–021–4
Printed in the United States of America

PUBLISHER'S NOTE

This collection of inspiring thoughts has been taken chiefly from the writings of Paramahansa Yogananda, founder in 1917 of Yogoda Satsanga Society of India and in 1920 of Self-Realization Fellowship in America, international headquarters of SRF-YSS.

His life's work was the dissemination of the spiritual science of *Kriya Yoga,* a technique of meditation whereby man may attain direct personal experience of God. Paramahansa Yogananda expounded the teachings of Bhagavan Krishna, the Christ of India, and of Lord Jesus, the Christ of the West, as in essence one. He taught that by conscious communion with the universal Christ Consciousness manifest in them, and in all God-realized avatars, mankind may know true brotherhood under the Fatherhood of God. Paramahansa Yogananda has shown thousands of spiritually aspiring men and women how they can commune, through *Kriya Yoga,* with that omnipresent Christ Consciousness which is the "light of the world."

In his writings Paramahansa Yogananda recorded many stories about the illustrious line of Self-Realization Fellowship masters: Mahavatar Babaji, Lahiri Mahasaya, and his own guru, Swami Sri Yukteswar. The SRF *Spiritual Diary* includes much wisdom from the lips of these great ones. Inspiring passages have also been chosen from the talks and letters of Rajarsi Janakananda and Sister Gyanamata, two highly advanced Western disciples of Paramahansa Yogananda.

Users of the *Diary* will find after each thought for the day the name of the person whose words are quoted, and the book or other publication from which it has been taken. Since the name of the person quoted may not necessarily be the author of the publication shown as the source, the following list is given for the reader's interest and convenience.

Paramahansa Yogananda is the author of these books: *Autobiography of a Yogi, Man's Eternal Quest, Whispers from Eternity, Sayings of Yogananda, Metaphysical Meditations, Scientific Healing Affirmations, The Law of Success,* and *How You Can Talk With God.* He is the author, also, of individually printed short sayings called *Para-grams,* and of the *SRF Lessons,* which are compiled from his writings and talks to students. For complete information about the foregoing, inquiry should be made to Self-Realization Fellowship headquarters in Los Angeles.

SELF-REALIZATION FELLOWSHIP

3880 San Rafael Avenue
Los Angeles, California 90065

PREFACE

By Sri Daya Mata

President, Self-Realization Fellowship
(Yogoda Satsanga Society of India)

"For as he thinketh in his heart, so is he" (Proverbs 23:7). This wisdom may be heeded by every man who would improve himself and strive to realize the highest goal of life: God. What we consistently think about will influence what we become. Our circumstances in life, our moods and habits, our successes and failures, are largely products of our thoughts. Indeed, the power of mind is the originating and governing force behind all creation.

Training the mind to dwell on positive, inspiring thoughts helps one to concentrate his energies for the accomplishment of a definite and lasting objective. I learned to apply this spiritual science years ago under the guidance of my great guru, Paramahansa Yogananda. To take even one facet of Truth each day and dwell upon it, and strive to live by it, has a miraculously transforming effect on one's inner and outer life. Never begin a day without first anchoring the mind to some guiding principle of Truth.

We easily become caught up in material duties and forget our spiritual responsibilities. We slave for the body; but what of our duty to the soul? That image of God within us cries to express its Spirit-qualities: eternal life, immeasurable divine love and wisdom, boundless joy. All that God is, and has, is ours by divine birthright. To know this is Self-realization.

In this *Spiritual Diary* are inspiring thoughts to guide you each day of the year. If you apply them in all your endeavors, material or spiritual, your actions will be surcharged with divine power. Think truth, think good, think God. If your mind is filled with His light, there can be no darkness for you.

HOW TO USE THIS "SPIRITUAL DIARY"

This Diary is intended as a daily guide to spiritual thinking, the foundation of spiritual living. Thoughts for special annual occasions that have fixed dates of commemoration are shown under the traditional date; where the date varies each year (for example, Easter), the special thought for that day appears on a separate page preceding the month in which it usually falls.

Each morning read the thought for the day. Then sit quietly and meditate upon the thought to absorb its meaning. Ponder its application in your own life. Strive to attune your mind to the deep spiritual perception and vitality that brought these words into manifestation.

During the day recall the thought as often as you can: repeat it mentally with deep concentration; or repeat it aloud, if circumstances permit. Strive in as many ways as you can to make that idea work for you and others in a practical way.

At night before retiring, mentally repeat the thought again, and record in this *Spiritual Diary* some of your own spiritual observations and self-analysis.

By deeply dwelling on the truths contained in this *Diary* and by striving to practice the message each thought contains, you will find your consciousness and your daily life subtly transformed. Right thoughts are the springboard of right action; right action leads to inner peace and lasting happiness, and to the gradual unfoldment of your own Self-realization.

With the opening of the New Year, all the closed portals of limitations will be thrown open and I shall move through them to vaster fields, where my worthwhile dreams of life will be fulfilled.—*Paramahansa Yogananda, "Self-Realization Magazine"*

For the New Year my greatest wish and prayer for you is that you cast aside wrong habits of thinking and doing. Don't drag your bad habits into the New Year. You don't have to carry them with you. Any minute you may have to drop your mortal package, and those habits will vanish. They don't belong to you now. Don't admit them! Leave behind all useless thoughts and past sorrows and bad habits. Start life anew!—*Paramahansa Yogananda, "Self-Realization Magazine"*

Choose which habits you are going to destroy in the New Year. Make up your mind about them and stick to your decision. Resolve to give more time to God: to meditate regularly every day, and on one night each week to meditate several hours, so that you can feel your spiritual progress in God. Resolve that you are going to practice *Kriya Yoga* regularly and that you are going to control your appetites and emotions. Be a master!—*Paramahansa Yogananda, "Man's Eternal Quest"*

In the beginning of one's spiritual search, it is wise to compare various spiritual paths and teachers. But when you find the real guru destined for you, the one whose teachings can lead you to the Divine Goal, then restless searching should cease. A spiritually thirsty person should not go on indefinitely seeking new wells; rather he should go to the best well and drink daily of its living waters.—*Paramahansa Yogananda, SRF Lessons*

Birthday of Paramahansa Yogananda

If I don't see you, remember I am working for you in some other place. My seeing you all the time will not necessarily help you. You will receive more by meditating deeply and regularly. I am not here only to help you in this life, but in the beyond also.
—*Paramahansa Yogananda, Lecture*

I want to ply my boat, many times,
Across the gulf-after-death,
And return to earth's shores from my home in Heaven.
I want to load my boat
With those waiting, thirsty ones who are left behind,
And carry them by the opal pool of iridescent joy
Where my Father distributes
His all-desire-quenching liquid peace.

> —*Paramahansa Yogananda,*
> *"Man's Eternal Quest"*

O my Guru! If all the gods are wroth, and yet thou art satisfied with me, I am safe in the fortress of thy pleasure. And if all the gods protect me by the parapets of their blessings, and yet I receive not thy benediction, I am an orphan, left to pine spiritually in the ruins of thy displeasure.—*Paramahansa Yogananda, "Whispers from Eternity"*

It is because God wants you that I am here with you, calling you to come Home, where my Beloved is, where Christ and Krishna, and Babaji, Lahiri Mahasaya, Sri Yukteswarji, and the other saints are. "Come," the Lord is saying, "they are all rejoicing in Me. No worldly joys—the taste of food, the beauty of flowers, the passing pleasure of earthly love—can compare with the divine joys of My home."

There is only one Reality. It is He. Forget everything else.—*Paramahansa Yogananda, "Sayings of Yogananda"*

When one has found his guru there should be unconditional devotion to him, because he is the vehicle of God. The guru's sole purpose is to bring the disciple to Self-realization; the love a guru receives from a devotee is given by the guru to God.—*Paramahansa Yogananda, "Sayings of Yogananda"*

I never miss you all when I am away, because inwardly you are always with me now, and will be forevermore. Whether we are living here or pass through the portals of death, we shall always be together in God.—*Paramahansa Yogananda to a group of disciples*

Without a guru the average devotee cannot find God. It requires 25% devoted practice of meditation techniques; 25% blessings of the guru; and 50% grace of God. If you remain steadfast in your efforts to the end, He will appear before you.—*Paramahansa Yogananda, "Self-Realization Magazine"*

The true disciple obeys his guru implicitly in everything because the guru is a man of wisdom and purity.
—*Paramahansa Yogananda, "Self-Realization Magazine"*

If we allow our will to be led by the wisdom of a master, whose will is in tune with God's, the master then seeks to guide our will in such a way that we travel swiftly on the road back to divinity. The chief difference between a worldly man and a saint is that the wise man has attuned his will to the Divine Will.
—*Rajarsi Janakananda, "Rajarsi Janakananda: Great Western Yogi"*

Sometimes students say to me: "Such-and-such person is making better spiritual progress than I am. Why?" I reply: "He knows how to listen." All men would be able to transform their lives by hearing with deep attention the simple counsel given in the ethical code of all religions. It is the stony core of egotism in the hearts of most men that prevents their listening carefully to the wisdom of the ages.—*Paramahansa Yogananda, "Self-Realization Magazine"*

Obedience to the guru is necessary for attunement with his wisdom. It is not slavery to follow the wish of a God-realized guru, because his wish gives independence and freedom. A true guru is the servant of God, carrying out His plan for your liberation. Realize this, and you will always obey, until you find perfect freedom in Spirit.—*Paramahansa Yogananda, "Self-Realization Magazine"*

Without God-realization you have little freedom. Your life is ruled by impluse, whims, moods, habits, and environment. By following the advice of a true guru, and by accepting his discipline, you will gradually emerge from sense slavery.—*Paramahansa Yogananda, "Sayings of Yogananda"*

It is easy for me to plant the seed of love for the Divine in those who are in tune with me. Those who obey my wishes are in reality not obeying me but the Father in me. God doesn't talk to man direct, but uses the channel of the guru and his teachings.—*Paramahansa Yogananda, "Self-Realization Magazine"*

Even the greatest masters listen humbly to their gurus, because it is the way of righteousness.—*Paramahansa Yogananda, "Self-Realization Magazine"*

When you are unwilling to perform a task you are tired from the beginning, and when you are willing you are full of energy. Always work willingly and you will find that you are sustained by the indefatigable power of God.—*Paramahansa Yogananda, "Self-Realization Magazine"*

The secret of progress is self-analysis. Introspection is a mirror in which to see recesses of your mind that otherwise would remain hidden from you. Diagnose your failures and sort out your good and bad tendencies. Analyze what shortcomings are impeding you.—*Paramahansa Yogananda, "The Law of Success"*

Everyone should learn to analyze himself dispassionately. Write down your thoughts and aspirations daily. Find out what you are—not what you imagine you are!—because you want to make yourself what you ought to be. Most people don't change because they don't see their own faults.—*Paramahansa Yogananda, "Man's Eternal Quest"*

Endeavor to make yourself what you should be and what you want to be. As you keep your mind on God and attune yourself to His will, you will progress more and more surely in your path.—*Paramahansa Yogananda, "The Law of Success"*

It is a good idea to keep a mental diary. Before you go to bed each night, sit for a short time and review the day. See what you are becoming. Do you like the trend of your life? If not, change it.—*Paramahansa Yogananda, "Sayings of Yogananda"*

Many people excuse their own faults but judge others harshly. We should reverse this attitude by excusing others' shortcomings and by harshly examining our own.—*Paramahansa Yogananda, "The Law of Success"*

Anything of which you are cognizant has a relative vibration within yourself. One who is quick to see and judge evil in other persons has the seed of that evil within himself. The God-like person of pure and high vibrational tone is always aware of the God-spark in all he contacts, and his magnetic soul vibration draws to greater intensity that vibrational force in those who come within his vibrational range.—
Paramahansa Yogananda, SRF Lessons

If you find that every day you are becoming either touchy, finicky, or gossipy, then you know that you are going backward. The best test is to analyze yourself and find out whether you are happier today than you were yesterday. If you feel that you are happier today, then you are progressing; and this feeling of happiness must continue.—*Paramahansa Yogananda, SRF Lessons*

It is usually more or less easy to analyze others and classify them according to personality. It is often more difficult to turn the searchlight on one's self in strict honesty, but that is what you must do in order to find out what improvement or change is necessary. One purpose in discovering your own personality is to know how you affect others. Consciously, or unconsciously, people feel your personality, and their reaction is a clue.—*Paramahansa Yogananda, SRF Lessons*

Look within yourself. Remember, the Infinite is everywhere. Diving deep into superconsciousness, you can speed your mind through eternity; by the power of mind you can go farther than the farthest star. The searchlight of mind is fully equipped to throw its superconscious rays into the innermost heart of Truth. Use it to do so.—*Paramahansa Yogananda, "Man's Eternal Quest"*

You know when you are doing wrong. Your whole being tells you, and that feeling is God's voice. If you do not listen to Him, then He is quiet; but when you spiritually waken again He will guide you. He sees your good and your evil thoughts and actions, but whatever you do, you are His child just the same.
—*Paramahansa Yogananda, SRF Lessons*

I always remember this truth when I mentally try to find a way to escape from something that seems too hard for me. I think then: "I am escaping, not overcoming."—*Sister Gyanamata, "Self-Realization Magazine"*

By constantly following the inner voice of conscience, which is the voice of God, you will become a truly moral person, a highly spiritual being, a man of peace.—*Paramahansa Yogananda, Lecture*

Renunciation is the wise path trod by the devotee who willingly gives up the lesser for the greater. He relinquishes passing sense pleasures for the sake of eternal joys. Renunciation is not an end in itself, but clears the ground for the manifestation of soul qualities. No one should fear the rigors of self-denial; the spiritual blessings that follow are great and incomparable.—*Paramahansa Yogananda, "Self-Realization Magazine"*

To engage in actions without desire for their fruit is true renunciation. God is the Divine Renunciant, for He carries on all the activities of the universe without attachment to them. Anyone aspiring to Self-realization must act and live for the Lord without being emotionally involved in His drama of creation.— *Paramahansa Yogananda, "Self-Realization Magazine"*

The saints stress non-attachment so that one strong point of material attachment may not prevent our attaining the entire kingdom of God. Renunciation does not mean giving up everything; it means giving up small pleasures for eternal bliss.—*Paramahansa Yogananda, "How You Can Talk With God"*

Renunciation is not an end, it is the means to an end. The real renunciant is he who lives for God first, regardless of his outer mode of existence. To love God and conduct your life to please Him—that is what matters. When you will do that, you will know the Lord.—*Paramahansa Yogananda, "Man's Eternal Quest"*

At heart renounce everything, and realize that you are just playing a part in the intricate Cosmic Movie, a part that sooner or later must be over. You will then forget it as a dream. Our environment produces the delusion in us of the seeming importance of our present roles and our present tests. Rise above that temporal consciousness. So realize God within that He becomes the only influence in your life.— *Paramahansa Yogananda, "Rajarsi Janakananda: Great Western Yogi"*

A lazy person never finds God. An idle mind becomes the workshop of the devil. But persons who work without any desire for the fruits of action, desiring God alone, are true renunciants.—*Paramahansa Yogananda, "Self-Realization Magazine"*

It is all right to enjoy life; the secret of happiness is not to become attached to anything. Enjoy the smell of the flower, but see God in it. I have kept the consciousness of the senses only that in using them I may always perceive and think of God. "Mine eyes were made to behold Thy beauty everywhere. My ears were made to hear Thine omnipresent voice." That is Yoga, union with God. It is not necessary to go to the forest to find Him. Worldly habits will hold us fast wherever we may be until we free ourselves from them. The yogi learns to find God in the cave of his heart. Wherever he goes, he carries with him the blissful consciousness of God's presence.—*Paramahansa Yogananda, "Man's Eternal Quest"*

What I could not understand was why everything must go; why things that were right, that were mine, that harmed no one, why all the dear little rights and privileges must be taken from me. But they were so taken by God. He was thrusting me out of a life of dependence upon small comforts into one that should be lived for Him alone.—*Sister Gyanamata, "Self-Realization Magazine"*

Renunciation is not negative but positive. It isn't the giving up of anything except misery. One should not think of renunciation as a path of sacrifice. Rather it is a divine investment, by which our few cents of self-discipline will yield a million spiritual dollars. Is it not wisdom to spend the golden coins of our fleeting days to purchase Eternity?—*Paramahansa Yogananda, "Sayings of Yogananda"*

The Lord wants us to escape this delusive world. He cries for us, for He knows how hard it is for us to gain His deliverance. But you have only to remember that you are His child. Don't pity yourself. You are loved just as much by God as are Christ and Krishna. You must seek His love, for it encompasses eternal freedom, endless joy and immortality.—*Paramahansa Yogananda, "Self-Realization Magazine"*

The greatest romance is with the Infinite. You have no idea how beautiful life can be. When you suddenly find God everywhere, when He comes and talks to you and guides you, the romance of divine love has begun.—*Paramahansa Yogananda, "Man's Eternal Quest"*

The love of God is the only Reality. We must realize this love of God—so great, so joyful, I could not even begin to tell you how great it is! People in the world think, "I do this, I enjoy that." Yet whatever they are doing and enjoying inevitably comes to an end. But the love and joy of God that I feel is without any end. One can never forget it once he has tasted it; it is so great he could never want anything else to take its place. What we all really want is the love of God. And you will have it when you attain deeper realization.—*Rajarsi Janakananda, "Rajarsi Janakananda: Great Western Yogi"*

God will not tell you that you should desire Him above all else, because He wants your love to be freely given, without "prompting." That is the whole secret in the game of this universe. He who created us yearns for our love, He wants us to give it spontaneously, without His asking. Our love is the one thing God does not possess, unless we choose to bestow it. So, you see, even the Lord has something to attain: our love. And we shall never be happy until we give it.—*Paramahansa Yogananda, "How You Can Talk With God"*

He is the nearest of the near, the dearest of the dear. Love Him as a miser loves money, as an ardent man loves his sweetheart, as a drowning person loves breath. When you yearn for God with intensity, He will come to you.—*Paramahansa Yogananda, "Sayings of Yogananda"*

All my questions have been answered not through man but through God. He *is,* He *is.* It is His spirit that talks to you through me. It is His love that I speak of. Thrill after thrill! Like gentle zephyrs His love comes over the soul. Day and night, week after week, year after year, it goes on increasing. You don't know where the end is. And that is what you are seeking, every one of you. You think you want human love and prosperity, but behind it is your Father who is calling you. If you realize He is greater than all His gifts, you will find Him.—*Paramahansa Yogananda, Lecture*

Develop the love of God so that I see in your eyes that you are drunk with God and not asking, "When will I have God?" When you ask that, you are not a devotee. The devotee says: "I have Him, He is listening to me; my Beloved is always with me. He is moving my hands; He is digesting my food; He is gazing at me through the stars."—*Paramahansa Yogananda, Lecture*

If, in the darkness, the mind never wavers, if love and longing never grow weak, it is then that you prove to yourself that you really have the love of God.
—*Sister Gyanamata, "Self-Realization Magazine"*

When the Lord commanded: "Thou shalt have no other gods before me. Thou shalt not make unto thee any graven image" (Ex. 20: 3–4), He meant that we should not exalt the objects of creation above the Creator. Our love for Nature, family, friends, duties, and possessions should not occupy the supreme throne in our hearts. That is where *God* belongs.
—*Paramahansa Yogananda, "Sayings of Yogananda"*

God's love is so all-embracing that no matter what wrongs we have done, He forgives us. If we love Him with all our hearts He wipes out our *karma.*—*Paramahansa Yogananda, "Self-Realization Magazine"*

God understands you when everyone else misunderstands you. He is the lover who cherishes you always, no matter what your mistakes. Others give you their affection for a while and then forsake you, but He abandons you never.

In countless ways God is daily seeking your love. He does not punish you if you refuse Him, but you punish yourself. You find that "all things betray thee, who betrayest Me."—*Paramahansa Yogananda, "Sayings of Yogananda"*

The love of God cannot be described. But it can be felt as the heart is purified and made constant. As the mind and the feeling are directed inward, you begin to feel His joy. The pleasures of the senses do not last; but the joy of God is everlasting. It is incomparable.—*Paramahansa Yogananda, "Self-Realization Magazine"*

Pride is blinding, banishing the vision of vast-
ness possessed by greater souls. Humbleness is the
open gate through which the divine flood of Mercy
and Power loves to flow into recipient souls.—*Paramahansa Yogananda, SRF Lessons*

Humility comes from realizing that God is the Doer, not you. When you see that, how can you be proud of any accomplishment? Think constantly that whatever work you are performing is being done by the Lord through you.—*Paramahansa Yogananda, "Self-Realization Magazine"*

The greatest man is he who considers himself to be the least, as Jesus taught. A real leader is one who first learned obedience to others, who feels himself to be the servant of all, and who never puts himself on a pedestal. Those who want flattery don't deserve our admiration, but he who serves us has a right to our love. Isn't God the servant of His children, and does He ask for praise? No, He is too great to be moved by it.—*Paramahansa Yogananda, "Sayings of Yogananda"*

If your work in life is humble, do not apologize for it. Be proud because you are fulfilling the duty given you by the Father. He needs you in your particular place; all people cannot play the same role. So long as you work to please God all cosmic forces will harmoniously assist you.—*Paramahansa Yogananda, "The Law of Success"*

A little knowledge is a dangerous thing, for the devotee may feel vain and self-satisfied, ceasing to seek the profundities of the Divine. Only he who is free from the sense of self-importance becomes more and more spiritual until he is one with God. A humble devotee is lacking in vanity and pettiness.—*Paramahansa Yogananda, "Self-Realization Magazine"*

Humbleness is the manifestation of an under-standing heart, and sets an example of greatness for others to follow.—*Paramahansa Yogananda, SRF Lessons*

The rains of God's mercy cannot gather on mountaintops of pride, but flow easily into valleys of humbleness.—*Paramahansa Yogananda, "Sayings of Yogananda"*

O Creator of All! in the garden of Thy dreams let me be a radiant flower. Or may I be a tiny star, held on the timeless thread of Thy love as a twinkling bead in the vast necklace of Thy heavens.

Or give me the highest honor: the humblest place within Thy heart. There I would behold the creation of the noblest visions of life.—*Paramahansa Yogananda, "Whispers from Eternity"*

God does not talk directly to you. He manifests Himself to you through the channel of a guru and the guru's teachings. Disciples are those who allow themselves to be fully disciplined by the channel.—*Paramahansa Yogananda, "Self-Realization Magazine"*

Inherent in the Self-Realization Fellowship teachings and spiritual techniques are the help and blessings of the SRF line of Gurus. Devotees who conduct their lives according to SRF principles will be blessed with the hidden and open direction of the SRF Gurus.—*Paramahansa Yogananda, SRF Lessons*

The Masters, the Good Shepherds of this world, come down from their high places and give their lives to searching for disciples who are lost in the darkness. They find them in desolate and dangerous places, arouse them, lift them to a divine shoulder, and bear them with rejoicing to a safe place in the fold. They feed them with celestial food and give them living water to drink, of which, if a man eat and drink, he shall live forever. They give them power to become the sons of God. They give their own lives to the last ounce of flesh and the last drop of blood, for the redemption of the sheep who know their voice.

—*Sister Gyanamata, "Self-Realization Magazine"*

It is the duty of the guru and the disciple to be loyal to each other, not only in one life, but for many lives if these are necessary to reach God. Those who are one hundred percent loyal to a guru can be sure of ultimate liberation and ascension. One may have many teachers, but only one guru, who remains as one's guru even in many different lives, until the disciple reaches the final goal of emancipation in God. You must remember this, once that relationship is formed.—*Paramahansa Yogananda, SRF Lessons*

The spiritual training Master has given me has been, and is, perfect. The Guru cannot be judged, if he is to be judged at all, by the rules that apply to a friendship between equals. I have always known this.—*Sister Gyanamata, "Self-Realization Magazine"*

The friendship that exists between guru and disciple is eternal. There is complete surrender, there is no compulsion, when a disciple accepts the guru's training.—*Paramahansa Yogananda, "Man's Eternal Quest"*

Mahasamadhi of Paramahansa Yogananda

My body shall pass but my work shall go on. And my spirit shall live on. Even when I am taken away I shall work with you all for the deliverance of the world with the message of God. Prepare yourselves for the glory of God. Charge yourselves with the flame of Spirit.—*Paramahansa Yogananda, SRF Lessons*

Swami Sri Yukteswar to his disciple Paramahansa Yogananda: "I will be your friend from now to Eternity, no matter whether you are on the lowest mental plane or on the highest plane of wisdom.

"I will be your friend even if you should err, for then you will need my friendship more than at any other time."—*Swami Sri Yukteswar, in the SRF Lessons*

Mahasamadhi of Swami Sri Yukteswar

Swami Sri Yukteswar to Paramahansa Yogananda, before whom he appeared in the flesh on June 19, 1936, more than three months after his *mahasamadhi* (a great yogi's final conscious exit from the body): "Grieve not for me.... You and I shall smile together, so long as our two forms appear different in the *maya*-dream of God. Finally we shall merge as one in the Cosmic Beloved; our smiles shall be His smile, our unified song of joy vibrating throughout eternity to be broadcast to God-tuned souls!"—*Swami Sri Yukteswar, in "Autobiography of a Yogi"*

My Guru showed me how to use the chisel of wisdom to make myself into a fitting temple to receive God's Presence. Each man can do the same, if he follows the precepts of divinely illumined teachers.— *Paramahansa Yogananda, SRF Lessons*

Man, as an image of God, possesses within him the divine all-accomplishing power of will. To discover through right meditation how to be in harmony with the Divine Will is man's highest obligation.— *Paramahansa Yogananda, "The Law of Success"*

To create dynamic will power, determine to do some of the things in life that you thought you could not do. Attempt simple tasks first. As your confidence strengthens and your will becomes more dynamic, you can aim for more difficult accomplishments. Be certain that you have made a good selection, then refuse to submit to failure. Devote your entire will power to mastering one thing at a time; do not scatter your energies nor leave something half done to begin a new venture.—*Paramahansa Yogananda, "The Law of Success"*

When guided by error, human will misleads us; but when guided by wisdom, human will is attuned to the Divine Will. God's plan for us often becomes obscured by the conflicts of human life and so we lose the inner guidance that would save us from chasms of misery.—*Paramahansa Yogananda, "The Law of Success"*

Always be sure, within the calm region of your inner Self, that what you want is right for you to have, and in accord with God's purposes. You can then use all the force of your will to accomplish your object; keeping your mind, however, centered on the thought of God: the Source of all power and all accomplishment.—*Paramahansa Yogananda, "The Law of Success"*

Mind is the creator of everything. You should therefore guide it to create only good. If you cling to a certain thought with dynamic will power, it finally assumes a tangible outward form. When you are able to employ your will always for constructive purposes, you become the controller of your destiny.—*Paramahansa Yogananda, "The Law of Success"*

If you use all available outward means, as well as your natural abilities, to overcome every obstacle in your path, you will thus develop the powers that God gave you—unlimited powers that flow from the innermost forces of your being. You possess the power of thought and the power of will. Utilize to the uttermost these divine gifts!—*Paramahansa Yogananda, "The Law of Success"*

Whatever you make up your mind to do, you can do. God is the sum total of everything, and His image is within you. He can do anything, and so can you, if you learn to identify yourself with His inexhaustible nature.—*Paramahansa Yogananda, "Man's Eternal Quest"*

Strengthen your will power, so that you will not be controlled by circumstances, but will control them.
—*Paramahansa Yogananda, in a "Para-gram"*

Your part is to awaken your desire to accomplish your worthy objectives. Then whip your will into action until it follows the way of wisdom that is shown to you.—*Paramahansa Yogananda, SRF Lessons*

Will Power

Remember, in your will lies the almighty power of God. When a host of difficulties comes and you refuse to give up in spite of all obstacles; when your mind becomes "set," then you will find God responding to you.—*Paramahansa Yogananda, "How You Can Talk With God"*

It is not your passing inspirations or brilliant ideas so much as your everyday mental habits that control your life.—*Paramahansa Yogananda, "The Law of Success"*

Good habits are your best helpers; preserve their force by stimulating them with good actions. Bad habits are your worst enemies; against your will they make you do the things that hurt you most. They are detrimental to your physical, social, mental, moral, and spiritual happiness. Starve bad habits by refusing to give them any further food of bad actions.—*Paramahansa Yogananda, "Scientific Healing Affirmations"*

Good and bad habits both take time to acquire force. Powerful bad habits can be displaced by opposite good habits if the latter are patiently cultured.—*Paramahansa Yogananda, "Scientific Healing Affirmations"*

A bad habit can be quickly changed. A habit is the result of concentration of the mind. To form a new and good habit, just concentrate in the opposite direction.—*Paramahansa Yogananda, "Sayings of Yogananda"*

Through difficult daily lessons you will some-time see clearly that bad habits nourish the tree of unending material desires, whereas good habits nourish the tree of spiritual aspirations. More and more you should concentrate your efforts on success-fully maturing the spiritual tree, that you may some-day gather the ripe fruit of Self-realization.—*Para-mahansa Yogananda, "The Law of Success"*

Be careful what you choose to do consciously, for unless your will is very strong, that is what you may have to do repeatedly and compulsively through the habit-influencing power of the subconscious mind.
—*Paramahansa Yogananda, SRF Lessons*

Habits of thought are mental magnets that draw to you certain things, people, and conditions. Weaken a bad habit by avoiding everything that occasioned it or stimulated it, without concentrating upon it in your zeal to avoid it. Then divert your mind to some good habit and steadily cultivate it until it becomes a dependable part of you.—*Paramahansa Yogananda, "The Law of Success"*

True freedom consists in performing all actions —eating, reading, working, and so forth—in accordance with right judgment and choice of will, not in being compelled by habits. Eat what you should eat and not necessarily what you are used to. Do what you ought to do, not what your bad habits dictate.—*Paramahansa Yogananda, "Scientific Healing Affirmations"*

It is only when you discard your bad habits that you are really a free man. Until you are a true master, able to command yourself to do the things that you should do but may not want to do, you are not a free soul. In that power of self-control lies the seed of eternal freedom.—*Paramahansa Yogananda, "The Law of Success"*

Do not continue to live in the same old way. Make up your mind to do something to improve your life, and then do it. Change your consciousness; that is all that is necessary.—*Paramahansa Yogananda, "Self-Realization Magazine"*

If you are able to free yourself from all kinds of bad habits, and if you are able to do good because you want to do good and not merely because evil brings sorrow, then you are truly progressing in Spirit.—*Paramahansa Yogananda, "The Law of Success"*

THOUGHTS FOR THE EASTER SEASON

The Crucifixion

O Christ, beloved Son of God! Thy trial on the Cross was an immortal victory of humility over force, of soul over flesh. May thine ineffable example hearten us to bear bravely our lesser crosses.

O Great Lover of error-torn humanity! In myriad hearts an unseen monument has arisen to the mightiest miracle of love—thy words: "Forgive them, for they know not what they do."—*Paramahansa Yogananda, "Whispers from Eternity"*

The Resurrection

Heavenly Father, I am resurrected with Christ from the sepulcher of the flesh into Thine omnipresence. I am resurrected from the smallness of family affection into the grandeur of love for all Thy creatures. I am resurrected from ignorance into Thine eternal wisdom. I am resurrected from all worldly desires into a state of desire for Thee alone. I am resurrected from longings for human love; I yearn only for divine love. I am one with Christ, I am one with Thee.—*Paramahansa Yogananda, "Self-Realization Magazine"*

Compassion toward all beings (*daya*) is necessary for divine realization, for God Himself is overflowing with this quality. Those with a tender heart can put themselves in the place of others, feel their suffering, and try to alleviate it.—*Paramahansa Yogananda, "Self-Realization Magazine"*

O Lord of Compassion, teach me to shed tears of love for all beings. May I behold them as my very own—different expressions of my Self.

I easily excuse my own faults; let me therefore quickly forgive the failings of others. Bless me, O Father, that I not inflict on my companions unwelcome criticism. If they ask my advice in trying to correct themselves, may I offer suggestions inspired by Thee.—*Paramahansa Yogananda, "Whispers from Eternity"*

Every day, try to help uplift, as you would help yourself or your family, whoever in your environment may be physically, mentally, or spiritually sick. Then no matter what your part is on the stage of life, you will know that you have been playing it rightly, directed by the Stage Manager of all destinies.—*Paramahansa Yogananda, SRF Lessons*

Thy divine light is hidden in even the most vicious and gloom-shrouded man, waiting to shine forth under the proper conditions: the keeping of good company, and ardent desires for self-betterment.

We thank Thee that no sin is unforgivable, no evil insuperable; for the world of relativity does not contain absolutes.

Direct me, O Heavenly Father, that I awaken Thy bewildered ones to the consciousness of their native purity, immortality, and celestial sonhood.—*Paramahansa Yogananda, "Whispers from Eternity"*

I will behold the person who now considers himself as my enemy to be in truth my divine brother hiding behind a veil of misunderstanding. I will tear aside this veil with a dagger of love so that, seeing my humble, forgiving understanding, he will no longer spurn the offering of my goodwill.—*Paramahansa Yogananda, "Metaphysical Meditations"*

Let the ugliness of unkindness in others impel me to make myself beautiful with loving-kindness.

May harsh speech from my companions remind me to use sweet words always. If stones from evil minds are cast at me, let me send in return only missiles of goodwill.

As a jasmine vine sheds its flowers over the hands delivering ax blows at its roots, so, on all who act inimically toward me may I shower the blossoms of forgiveness.—*Paramahansa Yogananda, "Whispers from Eternity"*

May I not increase the ignorance of wrongdoers by my intolerance or vindictiveness. Inspire me to help them by my forgiveness, prayers, and tears of gentle love.—*Paramahansa Yogananda, "Whispers from Eternity"*

Seek to do brave and lovely things which are left undone by the majority of people. Give gifts of love and peace to those whom others pass by.—*Paramahansa Yogananda, SRF Lessons*

As the vital rays of the sun nurture all, so must you spread the rays of hope in the hearts of the poor and forsaken, kindle courage in the hearts of the despondent, and light a new strength in the hearts of those who think they are failures.—*Paramahansa Yogananda, in a "Para-gram"*

When God does not respond to your prayers, it is because you are not in earnest. You offer Him dry imitation prayers, which is no way to claim the Heavenly Father's attention. The only way to reach God through prayer is by persistence, regularity, and depth of earnestness. Cleanse your mind of all negation, such as fear, worry, anger; then fill it with thoughts of love, service, and joyous expectation. In the inner sanctum of your heart there must be one power, one joy, one peace—and that is God.—*Paramahansa Yogananda, in a "Para-gram"*

As you cannot broadcast through a broken microphone, so you cannot send out prayers through a mental microphone that has been disordered by restlessness. By deep calmness you should repair your mind microphone and increase the receptivity of your intuition. Thus you will be able to broadcast to Him effectively and to receive His answers.—*Paramahansa Yogananda, "The Law of Success"*

More than in any other relationship, we may rightfully and naturally demand a reply from Spirit in Its aspect as the Divine Mother. God is constrained to answer such an appeal; for the essence of a mother is love and forgiveness, no matter how great a sinner her child may be. It is the closest and most beautiful of all the relationships that the Lord has given us.—*Paramahansa Yogananda, "How You Can Talk With God"*

Though God hears all our prayers He does not always respond. Our situation is like that of a child who calls for his mother, but the mother does not think it necessary to come. She sends him a plaything to keep him quiet. But when the child refuses to be comforted by anything except the mother's presence, she comes. If you want to know God, you must be like the naughty baby who cries till mother comes.—*Paramahansa Yogananda, "How You Can Talk With God"*

When God's devotees pray to Him He knows if their hearts and minds are dry of devotion and whether their thoughts are dashing wildly everywhere; He does not respond to halfhearted calls. But to those devotees who day and night with utmost intensity pray and talk to Him, He does appear. To such devotees He will come without fail.—*Paramahansa Yogananda, "How You Can Talk With God"*

I was kneeling in prayer in the chapel—I was thinking of something that was coming into my life which filled me with apprehension. I knew it was not the will of God that I should be saved from the experience. Even at that moment it was moving toward me. Suddenly God told me the prayer He would listen to, and I said quickly: "Change no circumstance of my life, change me."—*Sister Gyanamata, "Self-Realization Magazine"*

The demand for the Lord's reply should be strong; a half-believing prayer is not sufficient. If you make up your mind: "He *is* going to talk with me"; if you refuse to believe differently, regardless of how many years He has not answered you; if you go on trusting Him, one day He will respond.—*Paramahansa Yogananda, "How You Can Talk With God"*

If you can just once "break bread" with the Lord, break His silence, He will talk often with you. But in the beginning it is very difficult; it is not easy to become acquainted with God, because He wants to be sure that you really desire to know Him. He gives tests to see if the devotee wants Him or something else. He will not talk with you until you have convinced Him that no other desire is hiding in your heart. Why should He reveal Himself to you if your heart is filled only with longings for His gifts?—*Paramahansa Yogananda, "How You Can Talk With God"*

The best course is to pray: "Lord, make me happy with awareness of Thee. Give me freedom from all earthly desires, and above all give me Thy joy that outlasts all the happy and sad experiences of life."
—*Paramahansa Yogananda, "Man's Eternal Quest"*

One answer will cover all your questions: Turn to God and fill your consciousness with the realization of His perfection. Let your weakness be dissolved in the worshipful thought of His strength. It is not necessary to explain things to God, for He knoweth your need before you speak, and is more ready to give than you are to ask. When you meditate, turn away from everything except the one absorbing thought of His overshadowing Presence. In this way you will become receptive.—*Sister Gyanamata, "Self-Realization Magazine"*

The superconscious law of success is put into operation through man's prayers and by his understanding of the Lord's omnipotence. Do not stop your conscious efforts or rely wholly on your own natural abilities, but ask divine aid in all you do.—*Paramahansa Yogananda, "Scientific Healing Affirmations"*

In a time of misfortune I heard Thy voice, saying: "The sun of My protection shines equally on thy brightest and thy blackest hours. Have faith and smile! Sadness is an offense against the blissful nature of Spirit. Let My life-transforming light appear through the transparency of smiles. By being happy, My child, thou dost please Me."—*Paramahansa Yogananda, "Whispers from Eternity"*

Remember that when you are unhappy it is generally because you do not visualize strongly enough the great things that you definitely want to accomplish in life, nor do you employ steadfastly enough your will power, your creative ability, and your patience until your dreams are materialized.—*Paramahansa Yogananda, SRF Lessons*

Happiness depends to some extent upon external conditions, but chiefly upon mental attitudes. In order to be happy one should have good health, a well-balanced mind, a prosperous life, the right work, a thankful heart, and above all, wisdom or knowledge of God.—*Paramahansa Yogananda*, *"The Law of Success"*

The laughter of the infinite God must vibrate through your smile. Let the breeze of His love spread your smiles in the hearts of men. Their fire will be contagious.—*Paramahansa Yogananda, SRF Lessons*

You have the power to hurt yourself or benefit yourself. If you do not choose to be happy no one can make you happy. Do not blame God for that! And if you choose to be happy, no one can make you unhappy....It is we who make of life what it is.—*Paramahansa Yogananda, SRF Lessons*

A strong determination to be happy will help you. Do not wait for circumstances to change, thinking falsely that in them lies the trouble.

Do not make unhappiness a chronic habit, thereby affecting yourself and your associates. It is blessedness for yourself and others if you are happy.

If you possess happiness you possess everything; to be happy is to be in tune with God. That power to be happy comes through meditation.—*Paramahansa Yogananda, "The Law of Success"*

Rather than be always striving for personal happiness, try to make others happy. In being of spiritual, mental, and material service to others, you will find your own needs fulfilled. As you forget *self* in service to others, you will find that, without seeking it, your own cup of happiness will be full.—*Paramahansa Yogananda, SRF Lessons*

Do not think that a little joy in silence is enough. Joy is more than that. For instance, suppose you are going to be punished by not being allowed to go to sleep when you are desperately in need of rest, and suddenly someone says: "All right, you may go to sleep now." Think of the joy you would feel just before falling asleep. Multiply that one million times! Still it would not describe the joy felt in communion with God.—*Paramahansa Yogananda, SRF Lessons*

Real happiness comes only when your will is guided by soul discrimination to choose good instead of evil, anytime, anywhere, because you truly want good for its own sake. Then you will be really free.—*Paramahansa Yogananda, SRF Lessons*

Daily I will seek happiness more and more within my mind, and less and less through material pleasures.—*Paramahansa Yogananda, "Scientific Healing Affirmations"*

SPECIAL THOUGHT FOR MAY

Mother's Day

In India we like to speak of God as Mother Divine, because a true mother is more tender and forgiving than a father. The mother is an expression of the unconditional love of God. Mothers were created by God to show us that He loves us with or without cause. Every woman is to me a representative of the Mother. I see the Cosmic Mother in all. That which I find most admirable in woman is her mother love.
—*Paramahansa Yogananda, "Man's Eternal Quest"*

The only way to attain salvation is to have complete loyalty to God. This dream of life will be taken away from you one day; the only thing that is real is the love of God. Nothing else; all are false dreams. Get away from them. Every minute I see how necessary that is. He has tied me to the SRF work, and so I tell Him: "I shall work for You alone." Then I feel within His supreme joy.—*Paramahansa Yogananda, "Self-Realization Magazine"*

You are in this house of God; and this is your house. You should be proud of the work and loyal to it, that the blessing of God may flow through you. He who is not loyal to his own organization and the work that God has sent is not loyal to God. Though I am so liberal, yet you see I regularly mention only my line of Gurus—Babaji, Lahiri Mahasaya, and Sri Yukteswar.—*Paramahansa Yogananda, Lecture*

Always associate with those who are loyal to God and the Great Gurus and you will find your life becoming the highest type of life. Be true to the truth of Self-Realization teachings and you shall find your life filled with the glory of Spirit, with the effulgence of the Almighty.—*Paramahansa Yogananda, Lecture*

I take a sacred vow: Never shall the sun gaze of my love sink below the horizon of my thought of Thee. Never will I lower the vision of my lifted eyes to place it on aught but Thee. Never will I do anything that reminds me not of Thee.—*Paramahansa Yogananda, "Whispers from Eternity"*

Birthday of Rajarsi Janakananda

Speaking before a convocation of Self-Realization Fellowship students in 1953, Rajarsi said:

"All that I have to give to you is the spirit of Master and of God. I have nothing more to say, nothing more to do except to carry out the wishes that Master had for this great movement. And what he is doing for you these days is not of me. I myself am only his 'little one' that he spoke of; and I shall never be more than a little one because it will always be Master, Paramahansaji, who is my life and my blessing to you all."—*Rajarsi Janakananda, "Rajarsi Janakananda: Great Western Yogi"*

True devotees may be called fanatical in their devotion to Him. The only right kind of fanaticism is loyalty to God—night and day, night and day, thinking of Him. Without this kind of loyalty it is impossible to find God. Those who never miss *Kriya*, and who sit long in meditation and pray intensely to God, will discover the longed-for Treasure.—*Paramahansa Yogananda, "Man's Eternal Quest"*

God is ever calling you through the flute of my heart. Follow the truth that God has sent through Self-Realization Fellowship and you shall be forever blessed. Falter no more, you who have heard these words. I urge upon you—forget Him not. Our bodies may perish, but let our souls forever blaze as eternal stars in the heart of God.—*Paramahansa Yogananda, "Self-Realization Magazine"*

You will find that everything will betray you if
you betray your loyalty to God. So let not one drop
of oil fall from the lamp of your attention in the sanc-
tuary of silence as you meditate each day; yet carefully perform your duties in the world.—*Paramahansa Yogananda, "Self-Realization Magazine"*

God is equally present in all, but He is most definitely expressed in the heart of the spiritually minded, loyal person who thinks only of Him. Through your loyalty to God you can establish your Oneness with Him. Loyalty attracts the Divine Attention. Thus when the storms of life gather, and the waves of trials buffet you, you can guide the boat of your life safely to the divine shores by realizing His omnipresence.—*Paramahansa Yogananda, in a "Para-gram"*

Birthday of Swami Sri Yukteswar

To keep company with the guru is not only to be in his physical presence (as this is sometimes impossible), but mainly means to keep him in our hearts and to be one with him in principle and to attune ourselves with him.—*Swami Sri Yukteswar, "The Holy Science"*

Remember that finding God will mean the funeral of all sorrows.—*Swami Sri Yukteswar, in "Autobiography of a Yogi"*

Saintliness is not dumbness! Divine perceptions are not incapacitating. The active expression of virtue gives rise to the keenest intelligence.—*Swami Sri Yukteswar, in "Autobiography of a Yogi"*

Attachment is blinding; it lends an imaginary halo of attractiveness to the object of desire.—*Swami Sri Yukteswar, in "Autobiography of a Yogi"*

To those ever attached to Me, worshiping Me with love, I impart that discriminative wisdom (*Buddhi Yoga*) by which they attain Me.—*Bhagavan Krishna, in the "Bhagavad-Gita"*

Your good habits help you in ordinary and familiar situations but may not suffice to guide you when a new problem arises. Then discrimination is necessary.

Man is not an automaton, and therefore cannot always live wisely by simply following set rules and rigid moral precepts. In the great variety of daily problems and events, we find scope for the development of good judgment.—*Paramahansa Yogananda, "Sayings of Yogananda"*

Don't advertise all your secrets in your desire to be honest. If you tell about your weaknesses to unscrupulous persons, they will have **great times** poking fun at you if on some future occasion they wish to hurt you. Why should you supply the "ammunition"? Speak and act in a way that will bring lasting happiness to yourself and others.—*Paramahansa Yogananda, SRF Lessons*

Loyalty to a spiritual custom without sincerity and conviction is hypocrisy. Loyalty to the spirit of a custom even without clinging to a form is wisdom. But loyalty neither to spiritual custom, nor principle, nor teacher is spiritual degeneration. Stand by God and His servant, and you will see His hand working through all things.—*Paramahansa Yogananda, "Self-Realization Magazine"*

Don't mentally review any problem constantly. Let it rest at times and it may work itself out; but see that you do not rest so long that your discrimination is lost. Rather, use these rest periods to go deep within the calm regions of your inner Self.—*Paramahansa Yogananda, "The Law of Success"*

Always keep your discrimination alive. Avoid those things that will not benefit you. And never pass your time in idleness.—*Paramahansa Yogananda, Lecture*

When man becomes a little enlightened he compares his experiences relating to the material creation, gathered in the wakeful state, with his experiences in dream; and, understanding the latter to be merely ideas, begins to entertain doubts as to the substantial existence of the former. His heart then becomes propelled to know the real nature of the universe and, struggling to clear his doubts, he seeks for evidence to determine what is truth. In this state man is called *Kshattriya*, or one of the military classes; and to struggle in the manner aforesaid becomes his natural duty, by whose performance he may get an insight into the nature of creation and attain the real knowledge of it.—*Swami Sri Yukteswar, "The Holy Science"*

He is wisest who seeks God. He is the most successful who has found God.—*Paramahansa Yogananda, "The Law of Success"*

It is not a pumping-in from the outside that gives wisdom. It is the power and extent of your inner receptivity that determines how much you can attain of true knowledge, and how rapidly.—*Paramahansa Yogananda, in a "Para-gram"*

It is not necessary to go through every kind of human experience in order to attain ultimate wisdom. You should be able to learn by studying the lives of others. Why become helplessly involved in an endless panorama of events in order to discover that nothing in this world can ever make you happy?
—*Paramahansa Yogananda, "Man's Eternal Quest"*

This life is a master novel, written by God, and man would go crazy if he tried to understand it by reason alone. That is why I tell you to meditate more. Enlarge the magic cup of your intuition and then you will be able to hold the ocean of infinite wisdom.

—*Paramahansa Yogananda, "Sayings of Yogananda"*

The greatest thing you can do to cultivate true wisdom is to practice the consciousness of the world as a dream. If failure comes, say: "It is a dream." Then shut off the thought of failure from your mind. In the midst of negative conditions, practice "opposition" by thinking and acting in a positive, constructive way.—*Paramahansa Yogananda, "Man's Eternal Quest"*

As you look upon creation, which appears so solid and real, remember always to think of it as ideas in the mind of God, frozen into physical forms.
—*Paramahansa Yogananda, SRF Lessons*

Your true personality begins to develop when you are able, by deep intuition, to feel that you are not this solid body but are the divine eternal current of Life and Consciousness within the body.—*Paramahansa Yogananda, "Man's Eternal Quest"*

The *rishis* wrote in one sentence profundities that commentating scholars busy themselves over for generations. Endless literary controversy is for sluggard minds. What more quickly liberating thought than "God is"—nay, "God"?— *Swami Sri Yukteswar, in "Autobiography of a Yogi"*

Therefore whosoever heareth these sayings of mine, and doeth them, I will liken him unto a wise man, which built his house upon a rock: And the rain descended, and the floods came, and the winds blew, and beat upon that house; and it fell not: for it was founded upon a rock.—*Jesus Christ, in the New Testament*

Every day you should sit quietly and affirm, with deep conviction: "No birth, no death, no caste have I; father, mother, have I none. Blessed Spirit, I am He. I am the Infinite Happiness." If you again and again repeat these thoughts, day and night, you will eventually realize what you really are: an immortal soul.—*Paramahansa Yogananda, "Man's Eternal Quest"*

Sorrow, illness, and failure are natural results of transgressions against God's laws. Wisdom consists in avoiding such violations and finding peace and happiness within yourself through thoughts and actions that are in harmony with your real Self. Govern your mind wisely by dwelling upon the positive aspects of life.

Do not be satisfied with drops of wisdom from scanty earthly sources; rather, seek wisdom without measure from God's all-possessing, all-bountiful hands.—*Paramahansa Yogananda, in a "Para-gram"*

SPECIAL THOUGHT FOR JUNE

Father's Day

In creating this universe God revealed two aspects: the masculine or fatherly, and the feminine or motherly. If you close your eyes and visualize vast, illimitable space, you become overwhelmed and enthralled—you feel naught but pure wisdom. That hidden, infinite sphere wherein there is no creation, no stars or planets—only pure wisdom—is the Father.
—*Paramahansa Yogananda, "Man's Eternal Quest"*

Fix your mind inwardly between the eyebrows [as in meditation] on the shoreless lake of peace. Watch the eternal circle of rippling peace around you. The more you watch intently, the more you will feel the wavelets of peace speading from the eyebrows to the forehead, from the forehead to the heart, and on to every cell in your body. Now the waters of peace are overflowing the banks of your body and inundating the vast territory of your mind. The flood of peace flows over the boundaries of your mind and moves on in infinite directions.—*Paramahansa Yogananda, "Metaphysical Meditations"*

Peace is found through surrender to good, through devotion. People who are loving, who practice stillness, and delight in meditation and good actions, are really peaceful. Peace is the altar of God, the condition in which happiness exists.—*Paramahansa Yogananda, SRF Lessons*

Live each present moment completely and the future will take care of itself. Fully enjoy the wonder and beauty of each instant. Practice the presence of peace. The more you do that, the more you will feel the presence of that power in your life.—*Paramahansa Yogananda, SRF Lessons*

The peaceful individual remains calm until he wants to work, then he swings into action; and as soon as he is through, he swings back to the center of calmness. You must always be calm, like the pendulum that is still, but ready to swing into action whenever necessary.—*Paramahansa Yogananda, SRF Lessons*

Affirm divine calmness and peace, and send out only thoughts of love and goodwill if you want to live in peace and harmony. Live a godly life yourself and everyone who crosses your path will be helped just by being with you.—*Paramahansa Yogananda, SRF Lessons*

To be controlled by moods is to be a part of matter. If you keep your mind on the resolve never to lose your peace, then you can attain godliness. Keep a secret chamber of silence within yourself, where you will not let moods, trials, battles, or inharmony enter. Keep out all hatred, revengefulness, and desires. In this chamber of peace God will visit you.
—*Paramahansa Yogananda, SRF Lessons*

When you have peace in every movement of your body, and peace in your thinking, and in your will power, and peace in your love, and peace and God in your ambitions, remember—you have connected God with your life.—*Paramahansa Yogananda, SRF Lessons*

Be honest with yourself. The world is not honest with you. The world loves hypocrisy. When you are honest with yourself you find the road to inner peace.
—*Paramahansa Yogananda, Lecture*

When we become filled with the joy of making others happy by giving them God-peace, then we shall know that God is expressing Himself through us.—*Paramahansa Yogananda, in a "Para-gram"*

Each time a swarm of worries invades your mind, refuse to be affected; wait calmly, while seeking the remedy. Spray the worries with the powerful chemical of your peace.—*Paramahansa Yogananda, in a "Para-gram"*

Every minute is eternity because eternity can be experienced in that minute. Every day and minute and hour is a window through which you may see eternity. Life is brief, yet it is unending. The soul is everlasting, but out of the short season of this life you should reap the most you can of immortality.
—*Paramahansa Yogananda, SRF Lessons*

Everything is God. This very room and the universe are floating like a motion picture on the screen of my consciousness....I look at this room and I see nothing but pure Spirit, pure Light, pure Joy. The picture of my body and your bodies and all things in this world are only rays of light streaming out of that one sacred Light. As I see that Light I behold nothing anywhere but pure Spirit.—*Paramahansa Yogananda, talking to disciples at SRF Hermitage, Encinitas, California*

Eternity yawns at me below, above, on the left and on the right, in front and behind, within and without.

With open eyes I behold myself as the little body. With closed eyes I perceive myself as the cosmic center around which revolves the sphere of eternity, the sphere of bliss, the sphere of omniscient, living space.
—*Paramahansa Yogananda, "Metaphysical Meditations"*

So long as we are immersed in body consciousness, we are like strangers in a foreign country. Our native land is omnipresence.—*Paramahansa Yogananda, "Sayings of Yogananda"*

I feel Him percolating through my heart, as through all hearts, through the pores of the earth, through the sky, through all created things. He is the eternal motion of joy. He is the mirror of silence in which all creation is reflected.—*Paramahansa Yogananda, "Metaphysical Meditations"*

Learn to see God in all persons, of whatever race or creed. You will know what divine love is when you begin to feel your oneness with every human being, not before.—*Paramahansa Yogananda, SRF Lessons*

The Ocean of Spirit has become the little bubble of my soul. Whether floating in birth, or disappearing in death, in the ocean of cosmic awareness the bubble of my life cannot die. I am indestructible consciousness, protected in the bosom of Spirit's immortality.—*Paramahansa Yogananda, "Metaphysical Meditations"*

One day I saw a big pile of sand on which a tiny ant was crawling. I said: "The ant must be thinking it is scaling the Himalaya mountains!" The pile may have seemed gigantic to the ant, but not to me. Similarly, a million of our solar years may be less than a minute in the mind of God.—*Paramahansa Yogananda, "Sayings of Yogananda"*

We should train ourselves to think in grand terms: Eternity! Infinity!—*Paramahansa Yogananda, "Sayings of Yogananda"*

I soar in the plane of consciousness above, beneath, on the left, on the right, within and without, everywhere, to find that in every nook of my space-home I have always been in the sacred presence of my Father.—*Paramahansa Yogananda, "Metaphysical Meditations"*

We must meditate to attain deep faith. After we have received the first contact of God, we should then seek to develop the contact into a greater and greater consciousness. That is what Jesus asked everyone to do. He wanted them to receive his omnipresent consciousness. And that is what Paramahansaji teaches. He brings us God and all he asks is that we receive.—*Rajarsi Janakananda, "Rajarsi Janakananda: Great Western Yogi"*

O Spirit, teach us to heal the body by recharging it with Thy cosmic energy, to heal the mind by concentration and cheerfulness, and to heal the disease of soul ignorance by the divine medicine of meditation on Thee.—*Paramahansa Yogananda, "Whispers from Eternity"*

Absolute, unquestioning faith in God is the greatest method of instantaneous healing. An unceasing effort to arouse that faith is man's highest and most rewarding duty.—*Paramahansa Yogananda, "Scientific Healing Affirmations"*

The Infinite Source is an infinite dynamo, continually pouring strength, happiness, and power into the soul. That is why it is so important to rely as much as you can upon the Infinite Source.—*Paramahansa Yogananda, SRF Lessons*

Mind is the chief factor governing the body. One should always avoid suggesting to the mind thoughts of human limitations such as sickness, old age, and death. Rather, the mind should constantly be told this truth: "I am the Infinite, which has become the body. The body, as a manifestation of Spirit, is the ever-youthful Spirit."—*Paramahansa Yogananda, SRF Lessons*

Obey God's hygienic laws. The mental hygiene of keeping the mind pure is superior to physical hygiene, but the latter is important, and should not be neglected. Do not, however, live by such rigid rules that the least deviation from your wonted habits upsets you.—*Paramahansa Yogananda, "Scientific Healing Affirmations"*

The body is a treacherous friend. Give it its due; no more. Pain and pleasure are transitory; endure all dualities with calmness, trying at the same time to remove yourself beyond their power. Imagination is the door through which disease as well as healing enters. Disbelieve in the reality of sickness even when you are ill; an unrecognized visitor will flee.—*Swami Sri Yukteswar, in "Autobiography of a Yogi"*

Stubborn mental or physical diseases always have a deep root in the subconsciousness. Illness may be cured by pulling out its hidden roots. That is why all affirmations of the conscious mind should be impressive enough to permeate the subconsciousness, which in turn automatically influences the conscious mind. Strong conscious affirmations thus react on the mind and body through the medium of the subconscious. Still stronger affirmations reach not only the subconscious, but also the superconscious mind —the magic storehouse of miraculous powers.—*Paramahansa Yogananda, "Scientific Healing Affirmations"*

"Physicians should carry on their work of healing through God's laws as applied to matter," Sri Yukteswar said. But he extolled the superiority of mental therapy, and often repeated: "Wisdom is the greatest cleanser."—*Paramahansa Yogananda, "Autobiography of a Yogi"*

I shall recognize all disease as the result of my transgressions against health laws and I shall try to undo the evil by right eating, by less eating, by fasting, by more exercise, and by right thinking.—*Paramahansa Yogananda, "Metaphysical Meditations"*

Freedom means the power to act by soul guidance, not by the compulsions of desires and habits. Obeying the ego leads to bondage; obeying the soul brings liberation.—*Paramahansa Yogananda, "Sayings of Yogananda"*

Before you act, you have freedom, but after you act, the effect of that action will follow you whether you want it to or not. That is the law of *karma*. You are a free agent, but when you perform a certain act, you will reap the results of that act.—*Paramahansa Yogananda, SRF Lessons*

Man's freedom is final and immediate, if he so wills; it depends not on outer but inner victories.—
Paramahansa Yogananda, "Autobiography of a Yogi"

Birthday of Sister Gyanamata

The way to freedom is through service to others. The way to happiness is through meditation and being in tune with God....Break the barriers of your ego; shed selfishness; free yourself from the consciousness of the body; forget yourself; do away with this prison house of incarnations; melt your heart in all, be one with all creation.—*Paramahansa Yogananda, SRF Lessons*

You don't know how fortunate you are to have been born as a human being. In that you are blessed more than any other creature. The animal is not able to meditate and have God-communion. You have your freedom to seek Him and you don't use it.— *Paramahansa Yogananda, "Man's Eternal Quest"*

The soul is bound to the body by a chain of desires, temptations, troubles, and worries, and it is trying to free itself. If you keep tugging at that chain which is holding you to mortal consciousness, some day an invisible Divine Hand will intervene and snap it apart, and you will be free.—*Paramahansa Yogananda, "Man's Eternal Quest"*

To be able to do whatever one pleases is not the real meaning of freedom of action. You should understand to what degree you are free, and how much you are influenced by bad habits. To be good just because it has become a habit to be good is not freedom, either. To be tempted is not sinfulness, but to be able to resist and overcome temptation is greatness; this is freedom, for you are acting by free will and free choice only.—*Paramahansa Yogananda, SRF Lessons*

When by discrimination and right action man
"roasts" all the seeds of evil tendencies stored in the
mind, each microscopic brain cell becomes a throne
for a brilliant king of wisdom, inspiration, and health,
who sings and preaches the glory of God to the intel-
ligent body cells. Men who have attained this state
are really free. Such liberated beings are untouched
by *karma* in future incarnations, and reincarnate only
in order to wipe away the tears of the *karma*-bound.
These liberated masters are haloed in invisible healing light. Wherever they go, they scatter the light of
prosperity and health.—*Paramahansa Yogananda, SRF
Lessons*

Swami Sri Yukteswar to Paramahansa Yogananda: "Freedom of will does not consist in doing things according to the dictates of prenatal or postnatal habits or of mental whims, but in acting according to the suggestions of wisdom and free choice. If you tune in your will with mine [the wisdom-guided will of the guru], you will find freedom."—*Swami Sri Yukteswar, in SRF Lessons*

Resolve that you are not going to be affected by troubles; you are not going to be finicky; you are not going to be a victim of habits and moods; you are going to be free as a lark.—*Paramahansa Yogananda, "Self-Realization Magazine"*

You cannot be free unless you have burned the seeds of past actions in the fire of wisdom and meditation.—*Paramahansa Yogananda, "Self-Realization Magazine"*

I knew what I wanted long before I came [into the monastic Self-Realization Order]. I did not come for honor, nor for pleasure, nor for favor. I came for God. Some things surprised and disappointed me, but I moved on, from point to point, until I had the full vision of the Guru-disciple relationship. I saw that if the Master [had not disciplined me and instead] had treated me with what is called "kindness" I would never have known myself or my spiritual needs.—*Sister Gyanamata, "Self-Realization Magazine"*

Avoid a negative approach to life. Why gaze down at the sewers when there is loveliness all around us? One may find some fault in even the greatest masterpieces of art, music, and literature. But isn't it better to enjoy their charm and glory?

Life has a bright side and a dark side, for the world of relativity is composed of light and shadows. If you permit your thoughts to dwell on evil, you yourself will become ugly. Look only for the good in everything, that you absorb the quality of beauty.
—*Paramahansa Yogananda, "Sayings of Yogananda"*

I do not expect anything from others, so their actions cannot be in opposition to wishes of mine.—*Swami Sri Yukteswar, in "Autobiography of a Yogi"*

When you are told you are good, you should not relax but should try to become even better. Your continuous improvement gives happiness to you, to those around you, and to God.—*Paramahansa Yogananda, "Sayings of Yogananda"*

Don't concern yourself with the faults of others. Use the scouring powder of wisdom to keep the rooms of your own mind bright and spotless. By your example, other persons will be inspired to do their own housecleaning.—*Paramahansa Yogananda, "Sayings of Yogananda"*

Live only in the present, not in the future. Do your best today; don't look for tomorrow.—*Paramahansa Yogananda, "Self-Realization Magazine"*

Paramahansa Yogananda in a memorial tribute to Sister Gyanamata: "I had never seen, never heard Gyanamata criticize anybody; never heard a cross word from her lips. All the disciples whose good fortune it was to know her felt a new inspiration, and they all said: 'She is indeed a saint.'"—*Paramahansa Yogananda, "Self-Realization Magazine"*

These three instructions, plus meditation, contain the only rule of life that any disciple needs: detachment; realization of God as the Giver; and unruffled patience. As long as we fail in any one of these three, we still have a serious spiritual defect to overcome.—*Sister Gyanamata, "Self-Realization Magazine"*

If I were able to give you the gift that I would like best of all to offer you, it would be the right attitude toward God and Guru; toward life; toward your work; toward the others of your group.

But the best gifts cannot be purchased and given. The gifts and graces of the soul must be acquired by patient, daily practice. All will surely be yours in time, for if you do not obtain them in the position to which God has called you, where, in all the world, are they to be found?—*Sister Gyanamata, "Self-Realization Magazine"*

Once when I was meditating I heard His voice, whispering: "Thou dost say I am away; *but thou didst not come in*. That is why thou dost say I am away. I am always in. Come in and you will see Me. I am always here, ready to greet thee."—*Paramahansa Yogananda, "Self-Realization Magazine"*

When you meditate, immerse your whole mind in God. And when you are performing a duty, put your whole heart into it. But as soon as you are through with work, place your mind on the Lord. When you learn to practice the presence of God in every moment that you are free to think of Him, then even in the midst of work you will be aware of divine communion.—*Paramahansa Yogananda, "Self-Realization Magazine"*

Whenever your mind wanders in the maze of myriad worldly thoughts, patiently lead it back to remembrance of the indwelling Lord. In time you will find Him ever with you—a God who talks with you in your own language, a God whose face peeps at you from every flower and blade of grass. Then you shall say: "I am free! I am clothed in the gossamer of Spirit; I fly from earth to heaven on wings of light." And what joy will consume your being!—*Paramahansa Yogananda, "Sayings of Yogananda"*

God is approachable. Talking of Him and listening to His words in the scriptures, thinking of Him, feeling His presence in meditation, you will see that gradually the Unreal becomes real, and this world which you think is real will be seen as unreal. There is no joy like that realization.—*Paramahansa Yogananda, "Man's Eternal Quest"*

Mahavatar Babaji Commemoration Day

Mahavatar Babaji has promised to guard and guide all sincere *Kriya Yogis* in their path toward the Goal.... "Whenever anyone utters with reverence the name of Babaji," Lahiri Mahasaya said, "that devotee attracts an instant spiritual blessing."—*Paramahansa Yogananda, "Autobiography of a Yogi"*

Although I am planning and doing things in the world, it is only to please the Lord. I test myself: even when I am working I whisper within, "Where are You, Lord?" and the whole world changes. There is nothing but a great Light, and I am a little bubble in that Ocean of Light. Such is the joy of existence in God.— *Paramahansa Yogananda, "Man's Eternal Quest"*

How easily one can pack the day with foolishness, how difficult to fill it with worthwhile activities and thoughts! Yet God is not so much interested in what we are doing as in where the mind is. Everyone has a different difficulty, but God doesn't listen to any excuses. He wants the devotee's mind to be engrossed in Him in spite of any troublesome circumstances.—*Paramahansa Yogananda, "Self-Realization Magazine"*

Pray to Him, "Lord, You are the Master of creation, so I come to You. I will never give up until You talk to me and make me realize Your presence. I will not live without You."—*Paramahansa Yogananda, "Man's Eternal Quest"*

If you choose to see God, you can see Him everywhere. Whether you are washing dishes or digging a ditch or working in an office or a garden—whatever you may be doing, inwardly say: "Lord, manifest to me! You are right here. You are in the sun. You are in the grass. You are in this room. You are in my heart."
—*Paramahansa Yogananda, "Self-Realization Magazine"*

No matter which way you turn a compass, its needle points to the north. So it is with the true yogi. Immersed he may be in many activities, but his mind is always on the Lord. His heart constantly sings: "My God, my God, most lovable of all!"—*Paramahansa Yogananda, "Sayings of Yogananda"*

Whenever you see a beautiful sunset, think to yourself: "It is God's painting on the sky." As you look into the face of each person you meet, think within: "It is God who has become that form." Apply this trend of thought to all experiences: "The blood in my body is God; the reason in my mind is God; the love in my heart is God; everything that exists is God."—*Paramahansa Yogananda, SRF Lessons*

SPECIAL THOUGHT FOR JANMASHTAMI

Birthday of Bhagavan Krishna

The birthday of Krishna is celebrated according to the Indian lunar calendar. It falls on the eighth day of the waning moon between mid-August and mid-September.

He who seeth Me everywhere and seeth everything in Me, of him will I never lose hold, and he shall never lose hold of Me.

That yogi stays forever in Me, who, anchored in divine unity whatever his mode of existence, realizes Me as pervading all beings.

O Arjuna, the best type of yogi is he who feels for others, whether in grief or pleasure, even as he feels for himself.—*Bhagavan Krishna, in the "Bhagavad-Gita"*

The greatest of all duties is to remember God. The first thing to do in the morning is to meditate on Him and think how you can give your life to His service, so that all day long you will be filled with His joy.— *Paramahansa Yogananda, "Self-Realization Magazine"*

There is no way to find God's love other than to surrender to Him. Master your mind so that you may offer it to Him.—*Paramahansa Yogananda, "Self-Realization Magazine"*

Dear Father, whatever conditions confront me, I know that they represent the next step in my unfoldment. I will welcome all tests because I know that within me is the intelligence to understand and the power to overcome.—*Paramahansa Yogananda, "Metaphysical Meditations"*

If God were to say to me today: *Come home!* without a backward glance I would leave all my obligations here—organization, buildings, plans, people—and hasten to obey Him. Running the world is His responsibility. He is the Doer, not you or I.—*Paramahansa Yogananda, "Sayings of Yogananda"*

I am Thine, O Lord! I will make myself worthy of Thine acceptance. I will not make a burnt offering unto the Lord my God of that which cost me nothing. I will lay myself, with all my prejudices and pettiness, with all the flesh holds dear, upon the burning pyre.

I will lift my heart daily to Mahavatar Babaji, Lahiri Mahasaya, Swami Sri Yukteswarji, and my Guru Paramahansa Yoganandaji, asking for their many-jeweled gifts of Self-realization.

In the stillness of night, out of the depth of my heart, I will cry: "Speak, Lord, for Thy servant heareth."

When the call to disagreeable duty is sounded, I will answer: "Here am I, Lord, send me."—*Sister Gyanamata*, *"Self-Realization Magazine"*

May every act of my will be impregnated with Thy divine vitality. Ornament with Thy grace my every concept, every expression, every ambition. O Divine Sculptor, chisel Thou my life to Thy design!
—*Paramahansa Yogananda, "Whispers from Eternity"*

The Lord knows the course of our thoughts. He does not reveal Himself to us until we have surrendered to Him our last worldly desire; until each of us says: "Father, guide and possess me."—*Paramahansa Yogananda, "Sayings of Yogananda"*

When someone tells me how much he has worked for God, I see the poor quality of his spirit. Those who work for the Lord in the right way never think in terms of how much they are doing for Him. Rather, they think only of how much He is doing for them— giving them a body through which they can render service to others, a mind to think about Him and His wonders, and a heart to love Him as their Father, Maker, and sole Benefactor.—*Paramahansa Yogananda, "Self-Realization Magazine"*

No matter how hard you work, never go to bed without giving God the deepest attention. You won't die; but die for God if it is necessary.—*Paramahansa Yogananda, Lecture*

"Lord, my hands and feet are working for You. You have given me a certain part to play in this world, and everything I am doing in this world is for You." Surrender yourself to God and you will find that your life will become like a beautiful melody. If you try to do everything in the consciousness of God, you will see with joy that every day He is choosing certain duties for you to perform.—*Paramahansa Yogananda, Lecture*

Kriya Yoga is the real "fire rite" oft extolled in the *Gita*. The yogi casts his human longings into a monotheistic bonfire consecrated to the unparalleled God. ...All past and present desires are fuel consumed by love divine. The Ultimate Flame receives the sacrifice of all human madness, and man is pure of dross. His metaphorical bones stripped of all desirous flesh, his karmic skeleton bleached by antiseptic suns of wisdom, inoffensive before man and Maker, he is clean at last.—*Paramahansa Yogananda, "Autobiography of a Yogi"*

For the disciple to permit the thought that he is being unfairly treated to enter his mind is fatal. The will of God flows to the disciple through the Guru at all times. If we accept our discipline in the right spirit, it will strengthen our character as nothing else could.
—*Sister Gyanamata, "Self-Realization Magazine"*

Forsake slavery to the desires of the flesh. Until you have established your spiritual mastery over the body, the body is your enemy. Always remember that! Have no other desire than to spread His name and to think and sing of Him all the time. What joy! Can money give us this joy? No! It comes only from God.
—*Paramahansa Yogananda, "Self-Realization Magazine"*

The kingdom of my mind is begrimed with ignorance. By steady rains of diligence in self-discipline may I remove from my cities of spiritual carelessness the ancient debris of delusion.—*Paramahansa Yogananda, "Whispers from Eternity" (a book of prayers)*

...You cannot make steel until you have made the iron white-hot in fire. It is not meant for harm. Trouble and disease have a lesson for us. Our painful experiences are not meant to destroy us, but to burn out our dross, to hurry us back Home. No one is more anxious for our release than God.—*Paramahansa Yogananda, "Man's Eternal Quest"*

The aspiring yogi of the West as well as of the East must discipline himself similarly. He should refrain from making too much fuss about the body. If he sees he is finding time for everything else but is too busy for God, he should take the whip of discipline to himself. Why be afraid? There is everything to gain. If a man will not himself cry and struggle to attain his own salvation, will anyone else do it for him?—*Paramahansa Yogananda, "Man's Eternal Quest"*

In doing good we must sometimes suffer. To find the Lord we must be willing to suffer. What is it to endure discomfort of the flesh and discipline of the mind to gain the eternal solace of Spirit? Christ's joy in God was so great he was willing to give up the body for Him. The purpose of life is to attain that tremendous happiness—to find God.—*Paramahansa Yogananda, "Man's Eternal Quest"*

I have come to measure spiritual advancement, not alone by the light that surrounds one when he meditates or by the visions he has of saints, but by what he is able to endure in the hard, cold light of day. Christ's greatness was not only that he could go into meditation and gloriously realize his oneness with the Father, his absolute identity, but also that he could endure.—*Sister Gyanamata, "Self-Realization Magazine"*

Yoga is definite and scientific. Yoga means union of soul and God, through step-by-step methods with specific and known results. It raises the practice of religion above the differences of dogma. My guru, Sri Yukteswar, extolled Yoga; he did not, however, indicate that realization of God thereby would be immediate. "You have to work hard for it," he told me. I did, and when the promised results came, I saw that Yoga was marvelous.—*Paramahansa Yogananda, "Man's Eternal Quest"*

By meditation we connect the little joy of the soul with the vast joy of the Spirit. Meditation should not be confused with ordinary concentration. Concentration consists in freeing the attention from distractions and in focusing it on any thought in which one may be interested. Meditation is that special form of concentration in which the attention has been liberated from restlessness and is focused on God. Meditation, therefore, is concentration used to know God.
—*Paramahansa Yogananda, SRF Lessons*

Remember that the longer you practice meditation with intensity, the nearer you will be to joyous contact with the silent God. Intensity consists in making every today's meditation deeper than yesterday's and every tomorrow's meditation deeper than today's.—*Paramahansa Yogananda, SRF Lessons*

Do not say: "Tomorrow I will meditate longer." You will suddenly find that a year has passed without fulfillment of your good intentions. Instead, say:

"This can wait and that can wait, but my search for God cannot wait."—*Paramahansa Yogananda, "Sayings of Yogananda"*

The most destructive shaft of *maya*-delusion is un-
willingness to meditate, for by this attitude one prevents himself from tuning in with God and Guru.—
*Paramahansa Yogananda, "Rajarsi Janakananda: Great
Western Yogi"*

First things must come first. When you awaken in the morning, meditate. If you don't, the whole world will crowd in to claim you, and you will forget God. At night, meditate before sleep claims you. I am so strongly established in the habit of meditation that even after I lie down to sleep at night, I find I am meditating. I can't sleep in the ordinary way. The habit of being with God comes first.—*Paramahansa Yogananda, "Man's Eternal Quest"*

When you seek God, make even a short meditation so intense that it will seem you have spent hours
with Him.—*Paramahansa Yogananda, "Self-Realization
Magazine"*

The more you meditate, the more helpful you can be to others, and the more deeply you will be in tune with God. Selfish people remain spiritually hide-bound, but the unselfish expand their consciousness. When you find your omnipresence in meditation, you will find God. If He is pleased with you, all nature will work in harmony with you. Learn to talk to Him with all your soul.—*Paramahansa Yogananda, SRF Lessons*

Why should God surrender Himself easily to you? You who work so hard for money and so little for divine realization! The Hindu saints tell us that if we would give so short a time as 24 hours to continuous, uninterrupted prayer, the Lord would appear before us or make Himself known to us in some way. If we devote even one hour daily to deep meditation on Him, in time He will come to us.—*Paramahansa Yogananda, "Sayings of Yogananda"*

No matter what happens to your body, meditate. Never go to sleep at night until you have communed with God. Your body will remind you that you have worked hard and need rest, but the more you ignore its demands and concentrate on the Lord, the more you will burn with joyous life, like a globe afire. Then you will know that you are not the body.—*Paramahansa Yogananda, "Man's Eternal Quest"*

Do not lament if you see no lights or images in meditation. Go deep into the perception of Bliss; there you will find the actual presence of God. Seek not a part but the Whole.—*Paramahansa Yogananda, "Sayings of Yogananda"*

The more sweetening you put in water, the sweeter it becomes. Likewise, the longer you meditate intensely, the greater will be your spiritual advancement.—*Paramahansa Yogananda, SRF Lessons*

What joy awaits discovery in the silence behind the portals of your mind no human tongue can tell. But you must convince yourself; you must meditate and create that environment.—*Paramahansa Yogananda, SRF Lessons*

Everything in future will improve if you are making a spiritual effort now.—*Swami Sri Yukteswar, in "Autobiography of a Yogi"*

Practicing yoga is half the battle. Even if you don't feel enthusiastic in the beginning, if you go on practicing you will come to feel that tremendous longing for God which is necessary if you are to find Him.

Why don't you make the effort? Whence do all the beautiful things in creation continually emerge? Whence comes the intelligence of great souls, but from the storehouse of the Infinite Spirit? And if these wonders you see about you are not enough to induce you to seek Him, why should He reveal Himself to you? He has given you the capacity for love that you may yearn for Him above all else. Don't misuse your love and reason. And don't misuse your concentration and intelligence on false goals.—*Paramahansa Yogananda, "Self-Realization Magazine"*

Often we continue to suffer without making an effort to change; that is why we don't find lasting peace and contentment. If we would persevere we would certainly be able to conquer all difficulties. We must make the effort, that we may go from misery to happiness, from despondency to courage.—*Paramahansa Yogananda, "Man's Eternal Quest"*

To coax God to give Himself takes steady, unceasing zeal. Nobody can teach you that zeal. You have to develop that yourself. "You can take a horse to water but you cannot make him drink." Yet when the horse is thirsty it seeks out water with zeal. So, when you will not give importance to anything else—the tests of the world or the tests of the body—then He will come.—*Paramahansa Yogananda, "How You Can Talk With God"*

Those who do not give time to their religion cannot expect to know all at once about God and the hereafter. Usually people don't make the effort, or if they do, the effort is not deep and sincere enough. Nighttime should be spent with God. You sleep more than necessary, and thus waste many valuable hours. Night was meant to screen all the attractions of the world, that you might the more intently explore the kingdom of God.—*Paramahansa Yogananda, "Man's Eternal Quest"*

All souls are equal. The only difference between you and me is that I made the effort. I showed God that I love Him, and He came to me. Love is the magnet from which God cannot escape.—*Paramahansa Yogananda, "Sayings of Yogananda"*

I always believe that if I try just a little harder, I can bring about the conditions that seem just out of my reach. Remember that no one, not even a Master, can do *everything* for you. You have to do much yourself.—*Sister Gyanamata, "Self-Realization Magazine"*

Remember, if you don't find God, you are not making enough effort in your meditation. Should you not find the pearl after one or two divings, don't blame the ocean. Blame your diving; you are not going deep enough. If you dive really deep you will find the pearl of His presence.—*Paramahansa Yogananda, "Man's Eternal Quest"*

You should increase the strength of your body and then increase the strength of your mind. The best way to increase mental power is to try to accomplish something worthwhile every day. Choose some worthy task or project that you have been told you could not do, and try to do it. Each day strive to accomplish something that you have always thought you could not accomplish.—*Paramahansa Yogananda, SRF Lessons*

You should make a greater effort. Forget the past and trust more in God. Our fate is not predestined by Him; nor is *karma* the sole factor, though our lives are influenced by our past thoughts and past activities. If you are not happy with the way life is turning out, change the pattern. I don't like to hear people sigh and ascribe present failure to past-life errors; to do so is spiritual laziness. Get busy and weed the garden of your life.—*Paramahansa Yogananda, "Sayings of Yogananda"*

All the experiences I have told you about are scientifically attainable. If you follow the spiritual laws, the result is certain. If the result doesn't come, find fault with your effort. Intensity in all your religious practices is the only way. Those who don't meditate regularly and deeply are restless whenever they do meditate, and give up after a short effort. But if you make a greater effort day by day, the ability to go deep will come. I don't have to make any effort now; the whole world is gone instantly when I close my eyes and gaze into the Christ Center [the spiritual eye, in the forehead between the eyebrows].—*Paramahansa Yogananda, "Man's Eternal Quest"*

If your mind is fully identified with your activities, you cannot be conscious of the Lord, but if you are calm and receptive to Him within while being active without, you are rightly active.—*Paramahansa Yogananda, in a "Para-gram"*

You alone are responsible for yourself. No one else may answer for your deeds when the final reckoning comes. Your work in the world—in the sphere where your *karma,* your own past activity, has placed you—can be performed only by one person: yourself. And your work can be called a "success" only when in some way it serves your fellowman.—*Paramahansa Yogananda, "The Law of Success"*

Before embarking on important undertakings, sit quietly, calm your senses and thoughts and meditate deeply. You will then be guided by the great creative power of Spirit.—*Paramahansa Yogananda, "The Law of Success"*

Always perform small as well as important duties with deep attention, remembering that God is guiding and stimulating every worthwhile effort you are making to achieve a noble ambition.—*Paramahansa Yogananda, SRF Lessons*

I take on more and more work but I never feel I am overburdened, because I do everything for God.— *Paramahansa Yogananda, "Self-Realization Magazine"*

You came to earth to accomplish a divine mission [to be reunited with God]. Realize how tremendously important that is! Do not allow the narrow ego to obstruct your attainment of an infinite goal.
—*Paramahansa Yogananda, "Sayings of Yogananda"*

If we are at peace within our beings, we can harmoniously carry on our duties even in the business sphere. We can accomplish admirable things in the world without necessarily clashing with others. After our day's work is over we can retire within to be with God again. Eventually, even in the business world, we can perform all our duties with the full consciousness of God's presence. If we are calm and peaceful, come what may—success or seeming failure—we remain even-minded, feeling the certainty that His will is being done.—*Rajarsi Janakananda, "Rajarsi Janakananda: Great Western Yogi"*

Your new work should be your only concern now. Do not feel attachment to the old. Accept changes with equanimity, and perform in a spirit of divine freedom whatever duties come your way.—*Paramahansa Yogananda, "Sayings of Yogananda"*

First meditate and feel the divine Presence; then do your work saturated with the consciousness of God. If you do this you will never become tired. If you work for your Divine Beloved, your life will be filled with love and strength.—*Paramahansa Yogananda, SRF Lessons*

We will be seen on this stage of life again and again, until we become such good actors that we can play our parts perfectly, according to the Divine Will. Then the Stage Manager will say: "You need 'go no more out.' (Rev. 3:12). You have done My Will. You have played your part, and acted well. You did not lose courage. Now you have come back to Me, to be a pillar of immortality in the temple of My Eternal Existence."—*Paramahansa Yogananda, "Man's Eternal Quest"*

You are punishing the soul by keeping it buried, slumbering in matter life after life, frightened by nightmares of suffering and death. Realize that you are the soul. Remember that the Feeling behind your feeling, the Will behind your will, the Power behind your power, the Wisdom behind your wisdom is the Infinite Lord. Unite the heart's feeling and the mind's reason in a perfect balance. In the castle of calmness, again and again cast off identification with earthly titles, and plunge into deep meditation to realize your divine kingship.—*Paramahansa Yogananda, "Man's Eternal Quest"*

Don't waste time in seeking little things. Naturally it is easier to get other gifts from God than the supreme gift of Himself. But don't be satisfied with anything less than the highest.—*Paramahansa Yogananda, "How You Can Talk With God"*

If others fool away their time, you be lost in God. You will go ahead. Let your example change others' lives. Reform yourself and you will reform thousands.
—*Paramahansa Yogananda, "Rajarsi Janakananda: Great Western Yogi"*

Through the use of the *Kriya* key, persons who cannot bring themselves to believe in the divinity of any man will behold at last the full divinity of their own selves.—*Paramahansa Yogananda, "Autobiography of a Yogi"*

Mahasamadhi of Lahiri Mahasaya

At the morning hour of ten, one day after the body of Lahiri Mahasaya had been consigned to the flames, the resurrected master, in a real but transfigured body, appeared before three disciples, each of whom was in a different city.

"So when this corruptible shall have put on incorruption, and this mortal shall have put on immortality, then shall be brought to pass the saying that is written: Death is swallowed up in victory. O death, where is thy sting? O grave, where is thy victory? (I Corinthians 15:54–55)."—*Paramahansa Yogananda, "Man's Eternal Quest"*

One moon dispels the darkness of the heavens. Similarly, one soul who is trained to know God, a soul in whom there is true devotion and sincere seeking and intensity, will dispel the spiritual darkness of others wherever he will go.—*Paramahansa Yogananda, "Man's Eternal Quest"*

You should transfer your attention from failure to success, from worry to calmness, from mental wanderings to concentration, from restlessness to peace, and from peace to the divine bliss within. When you attain this state of Self-realization the purpose of your life will have been gloriously fulfilled.—*Paramahansa Yogananda, "The Law of Success"*

Meditate unceasingly, that you quickly behold yourself as the Infinite Essence, free from every form of misery. Cease being a prisoner of the body; using the secret key of *Kriya*, learn to escape into Spirit.
—*Lahiri Mahasaya, in "Autobiography of a Yogi"*

Birthday of Lahiri Mahasaya

I am ever with those who practice *Kriya*. I will guide you to the Cosmic Home through your ever enlarging spiritual perceptions. —*Lahiri Mahasaya, in "Autobiography of a Yogi"*

Mahavatar Babaji to Lahiri Mahasaya: "The millions who are encumbered by family ties and heavy worldly duties will take new heart from you, a householder like themselves....A sweet new breath of divine hope will penetrate the arid hearts of worldly men. From your balanced life, they will understand that liberation is dependent on inner, rather than outer, renunciations."—*Mahavatar Babaji, in "Autobiography of a Yogi"*

Not through a desultory life but through a regular and balanced life will you receive the blessings of the Masters. Then evil will never use you as an instrument.—*Paramahansa Yogananda, in a talk to disciples*

When you work for God, not self, it is just as good as meditation. Then work helps your meditation and meditation helps your work. You need the balance. With meditation only, you become lazy. With activity only, the mind becomes worldly and you forget God.—*Paramahansa Yogananda*, *"Sayings of Yogananda"*

Do not make unimportant things important, nor concentrate on trifles at the expense of vital matters, or you will hamper your progress. Impulsive actions that are not in keeping with one's real duties are undesirable. —*Paramahansa Yogananda, in a "Para-gram"*

Whether you are suffering in this life, or smiling with opulence and power, your consciousness should remain unchanged. If you can accomplish even-mindedness, nothing can ever hurt you. The lives of all great masters show that they have achieved this blessed state. —*Paramahansa Yogananda, "Man's Eternal Quest"*

I will be calmly active, actively calm. I will not become lazy and mentally ossified. Nor will I be overactive, able to earn money but unable to enjoy life. I will meditate regularly to maintain true balance.—*Paramahansa Yogananda, "Metaphysical Meditations"*

The material and the spiritual are but two parts of one universe and one truth. By overstressing one part or the other, man fails to achieve the balance necessary for harmonious development....Practice the art of living in this world without losing your inner peace of mind. Follow the path of balance to reach the inner wondrous garden of Self-realization.—*Paramahansa Yogananda, in a "Para-gram"*

Do not confuse understanding with a larger vocabulary. Sacred writings are beneficial in stimulating desire for inward realization, if one stanza at a time is slowly assimilated. Otherwise, continual intellectual study may result in vanity, false satisfaction, and undigested knowledge.—*Swami Sri Yukteswar, in "Autobiography of a Yogi"*

Though you must remain in the world, be not of the world. Real yogis can talk and mingle with people, but all the while their minds are rapt in God.—*Paramahansa Yogananda, SRF Lessons*

Millions of people live a one-sided life and pass on in incompleteness. God has given each of us a soul, a mind, and a body, which we should try to develop uniformly. If you have led a life dominated by worldly influences, do not let the world impose its delusions on you any longer. You should control your own life henceforth; you should become the ruler of your own mental kingdom. Fears, worries, discontent, and unhappiness all result from a life uncontrolled by wisdom. —*Paramahansa Yogananda, SRF Lessons*

Look fear in the face and it will cease to trouble you. —*Swami Sri Yukteswar, in "Autobiography of a Yogi"*

I know now that I am a lion of cosmic power. Bleating no more, I shake the error forest with reverberations of Thine almighty voice. In divine freedom I bound through the jungle of earthly delusions, devouring the little creatures of vexing worries and timidities, and the wild hyenas of disbelief.

O Lion of Liberation, ever send through me Thy roar of all-conquering courage.—*Paramahansa Yogananda, "Whispers from Eternity"*

Teach me to be tenaciously and cautiously courageous instead of often being afraid. I will fear nothing except myself, when I try to deceive my conscience.
—*Paramahansa Yogananda, "Metaphysical Meditations"*

In education not enough stress is laid upon the need for courage in the character. We must learn to *endure*. And the only way to learn is by enduring. In courage one sees the brilliant triumph of the soul over the flesh.—*Sister Gyanamata, "Self-Realization Magazine"*

Do not take life's experiences too seriously. Above all, do not let them hurt you, for in reality they are nothing but dream experiences....If circumstances are bad and you have to bear them, do not make them a part of yourself. Play your part in life, but never forget it is only a role. What you lose in the world will not be a loss to your soul. Trust in God and destroy fear, which paralyzes all efforts to succeed and attracts the very thing you fear.—*Paramahansa Yogananda, in a "Para-gram"*

I laugh at all fears, for my Father-Mother, beloved God, is attentively awake and present everywhere with the deliberate purpose of protecting me from the temptations of evil.—*Paramahansa Yogananda, "Metaphysical Meditations"*

Fearlessness means faith in God: faith in His protection, His justice, His wisdom, His mercy, His love, and His omnipresence....To be fit for Self-realization a man must be fearless.—*Paramahansa Yogananda, "Self-Realization Magazine"*

The wise devotee should be cautious, rather than afraid. He should cultivate a courageous spirit, without rashly exposing himself to conditions that may arouse apprehensions.—*Paramahansa Yogananda, "Self-Realization Magazine"*

I have bled for Thy Name; and for Thy Name's sake I am willing ever to bleed. Like a mighty warrior, with gory limbs, injured body, wounded honor, and a thorn crown of derision, undismayed I fight on. My scars I wear as roses of courage, of inspiration to persevere in the battle against evil.

I may continue to suffer blows on my arms outstretched to help others, and receive persecution instead of love, but my soul shall ever bask in the sunshine of Thy blessings, O Lord. Thou dost guide Thy soldier's campaigns that conquer for Thee the lands of human hearts now oppressed by sadness. —*Paramahansa Yogananda, "Whispers from Eternity"*

Fear nothing else, but try to fear fear....Remember, no matter what your tests are, you are not too weak to fight. God will not suffer you to be tempted more than you are able to bear.—*Paramahansa Yogananda, "Self-Realization Magazine"*

The worst of all temptations is restlessness. It is evil because it keeps your attention on the world and thus causes you to remain in ignorance of God. If you meditate regularly, you will be with God all the time.
—*Paramahansa Yogananda, SRF Lessons*

Evil has its power. If you side with it, it will hold you. When you make a misstep, return immediately to the ways of righteousness.—*Paramahansa Yogananda*, *"Sayings of Yogananda"*

When you permit temptation to overcome you, your wisdom is a prisoner. The quickest way to banish temptation is first to say "no" and get out of that particular environment; then reason it out later when calmness and wisdom return.—*Paramahansa Yogananda, SRF Lessons*

Desires are the most unrelenting enemies of man; he cannot appease them. Have only one desire: to know God. Satisfying the sensory desires cannot satisfy you, because you are not the senses. They are only your servants, not your Self.—*Paramahansa Yogananda, "Sayings of Yogananda"*

Temptation is not our own creation; it belongs to the world of *maya* (illusion), and all men are subject to it. But to enable us to free ourselves, God gave us reason, conscience, and will power.—*Paramahansa Yogananda, "Self-Realization Magazine"*

Doing something wrong from a moral or material standpoint is not the only meaning of temptation. Forgetting your soul by becoming too engrossed in the body and its comforts is temptation too.—*Paramahansa Yogananda, SRF Lessons*

Temptation is a sugarcoated poison; it tastes delicious; but death is certain. The happiness that people look for in this world does not endure. Divine Joy is eternal. Yearn for that which is lasting, and be hardhearted about rejecting the impermanent pleasures of this life. You have to be that way. Don't let this world rule you. Never forget that the Lord is the only reality....Your true happiness lies in your experience of Him.—*Paramahansa Yogananda, "Man's Eternal Quest"*

Shall you be better able to fight [bad habits] tomorrow than today? Why add today's mistakes to yesterday's? You have to turn to God sometime, so isn't it better to do it now? Just give yourself to Him and say: "Lord, naughty or good, I am Your child. You must take care of me." If you keep on trying, you will improve. "A saint is a sinner who never gave up."
—*Paramahansa Yogananda, "Sayings of Yogananda"*

Remember that as a child of God you are endowed with greater strength to overcome than you will ever need for all the trials that God may send you.—*Paramahansa Yogananda, "Self-Realization Magazine"*

The old orthodox way is to deny temptation, to suppress it. But you must learn to *control* temptation. It is not a sin to be tempted. Even though you are boiling with temptation, you are not evil; but if you yield to that temptation you are caught temporarily by the power of evil. You must erect about yourself protecting parapets of wisdom. There is no stronger force that you can employ against temptation than wisdom. Complete understanding will bring you to the point where nothing can tempt you to actions that promise pleasure but in the end will only hurt you. —*Paramahansa Yogananda, SRF Lessons*

When by our wrong thoughts we fall into the pit of error, we should pray: "Father, leave us not here, but pull us out through the force of our reason and will. And when we are out, if it is Thy will to test us further, first make Thyself known to us—that we may realize that Thou art more tempting than temptation."
—*Paramahansa Yogananda*, *"Man's Eternal Quest"*

SPECIAL THOUGHT FOR NOVEMBER

Thanksgiving Day

For your many blessings be thankful *every day*, not only when the calendar indicates Thanksgiving-time. The basis for your gratitude should not be material prosperity. Whether your worldly possesions be many or few, you are still rich in gifts from God. Love Him, not for the outward things He may give you but for His gift to you of Himself as your Father.

—*Paramahansa Yogananda, "Self-Realization Magazine"*

In the spiritual life one becomes just like a little child—without resentment, without attachment, full of life and joy.—*Paramahansa Yogananda, "Sayings of Yogananda"*

I sing a hymn unuttered by any other voice....To Thee, O Spirit, I give no intellectual, premeditated, and disciplined aria; only the untutored strains of my heart. For Thee no hothouse flowers, watered by careful emotions; only rare wild blossoms that grow spontaneously on the highest tracts of my soul.—*Paramahansa Yogananda, "Whispers from Eternity"*

Why do you consider nonessentials so important? Most people concentrate on breakfast, lunch, and dinner, work, social activities, and so on. Make your life more simple and put your whole mind on the Lord.—*Paramahansa Yogananda, "How You Can Talk With God"*

It is not wrong to tell the Lord that we want something, but it shows greater faith if we simply say: "Heavenly Father, I know that Thou dost anticipate my every need. Sustain me according to Thy will."— *Paramahansa Yogananda*, *"Sayings of Yogananda"*

You think you must have this or that and then you can be happy. But no matter how many of your desires are satisfied, you never will find happiness through them. The more you have, the more you want. Learn to live simply. Lord Krishna said: "His mind is full with contentment whose desires ever flow inward. That man is like a changeless ocean which is kept brimful with constantly entering waters. He is not a *muni* who bores holes of desires in his reservoir of peace and lets the waters escape."— *Paramahansa Yogananda, "Man's Eternal Quest"*

My Guru Sri Yukteswarji was reluctant to discuss the superphysical realms. His only "marvelous" aura was that of perfect simplicity. In conversations he avoided startling references; in action he was freely expressive.—*Paramahansa Yogananda, "Autobiography of a Yogi"*

God has proven that when He is with me all the "necessities of life" become unnecessary. In that consciousness you become more healthy than the average person, more joyous, more bountiful in every way. Don't seek little things; they will divert you from God. Start your experiment now: make life simple and be a king.—*Paramahansa Yogananda, "Man's Eternal Quest"*

Everything has its place, but when you waste time at the cost of your true happiness it is not good. I dropped every unnecessary activity so that I could meditate and try to know God, so that I could day and night be in His divine consciousness.—*Paramahansa Yogananda, "Self-Realization Magazine"*

We make too much of feeling, even admitting that the right kind of feeling is very enjoyable. What does it matter how you feel? Bear your lot so long as it is the will of God that you should do so. Act rightly, and in due time the right feeling of peace and joy will come.
—*Sister Gyanamata, "Self-Realization Magazine"*

It is so wonderful to be in tune with God and to trust in Him implicitly, being content wherever He places you and whatever He makes of you, accepting all with humility and devotion.—*Paramahansa Yogananda, "Self-Realization Magazine"*

Get devotion! Remember the words of Jesus: "Father, thou hast hid these things from the wise and prudent, and hast revealed them unto babes."—*Paramahansa Yogananda, "Sayings of Yogananda"*

God says: "To the devotional call of that child of Mine who struggles, prays, and meditates in order to know Me in body, mind, and soul as the all-pervading, ever-new Joy—as the ever-increasing Bliss of meditation—I silently and deeply respond."—*Paramahansa Yogananda, SRF Lessons*

When God's devotees pray to Him He knows whether their hearts and minds are dry of devotion and whether their thoughts are dashing wildly everywhere; He does not respond to halfhearted calls. But to those devotees who day and night with utmost intensity pray and talk to Him, He does appear. To such devotees He comes without fail.—*Paramahansa Yogananda, "How You Can Talk With God"*

Remember, in your will is the will of God. In your heart you must love nothing more than God, who is a "jealous" God. If you want Him, you must have the will to cast away from your heart every desire but the desire for Him.—*Paramahansa Yogananda, SRF Lessons*

Prayer in which your very soul is burning with desire for God is the only effectual prayer. You have prayed like that at some time, no doubt; perhaps when you wanted something very badly, or urgently needed money—then you burned up the ether with your desire. That is how you must feel for God. Talk to Him day and night; you will see that He will respond.

—*Paramahansa Yogananda, "Man's Eternal Quest"*

He who created us yearns for our love. He wants us to give it spontaneously, without His asking. Our love is the one thing God does not possess, unless we choose to bestow it. So, you see, even the Lord has something to attain: our love. And we shall never be happy until we give it.—*Paramahansa Yogananda, "How You Can Talk With God"*

You should not concentrate on the thought that you lack devotion, but should work to develop it. Why be upset because God has not shown Himself to you? Think of the long time you ignored Him. Meditate more; go deep....By changing your habits you will awaken in your heart the memory of His wondrous Being; and, knowing Him, there is no doubt that you will love Him.—*Paramahansa Yogananda, "Sayings of Yogananda"*

The true devotee's heart is always saying: "My Lord, my Lord, I do not want to become ensnared in the delusory drama of Thy creation. I want no part of it except to help in establishing Thy temple in the souls of men. My heart, my soul, my body and mind —everything belongs to Thee." Such devotion reaches God. That devotee knows God.—*Paramahansa Yogananda, "Self-Realization Magazine"*

Let not anyone else know how deeply you feel for the Lord. The Master of the Universe knows of your love; don't display it before others, or you may lose it.—*Paramahansa Yogananda, "Man's Eternal Quest"*

The Lord is found through unceasing devotion. When you want only the Giver, and not His gifts, then He will come to you.—*Paramahansa Yogananda, "Self-Realization Magazine"*

Every day should be a day of thanksgiving for the gifts of life: sunshine, water, and the luscious fruits and greens that are indirect gifts of the Great Giver. God makes us work so that we may deserve to receive His gifts. The All-Sufficient One does not need our thanks, however heartfelt, but when we are grateful to Him our attention is concentrated, for our highest benefit, upon the Great Source of all supply.—*Paramahansa Yogananda, "Self-Realization Magazine"*

Our dear ones promise to love us forever; yet when they sink into the Great Sleep, their earth memories forsaken, what value their vows? Who, without telling us in words, loves us everlastingly? Who remembers us when all others forget us? Who will still be with us when we must leave the friends of this world? God alone.—*Paramahansa Yogananda*, *"Whispers from Eternity"*

When the summer of good fortune warms my tree of life, it easily burgeons with fragrant blossoms of thankfulness. During winter months of misfortune, O Lord, may my denuded branches changelessly waft toward Thee a secret scent of gratitude.—*Paramahansa Yogananda, "Whispers from Eternity"*

Thanksgiving and praise open in your consciousness the way for spiritual growth and supply to come to you. Spirit pushes itself out into visible manifestation as soon as a channel is opened through which it can flow. You should be thankful for everything at all times. Realize that all power to think, and speak, and act comes from God, and that He is with you now, guiding and inspiring you.—*Paramahansa Yogananda, "Thanksgiving Message"*

In one of His aspects, a very touching aspect, the Lord may be said to be a beggar. He yearns for our attention. The Master of the Universe, at whose glance all stars, suns, moons, and planets quiver, is running after man and saying: "Won't you give Me your affection? Don't you love Me, the Giver, more than the things I have made for you? Won't you seek Me?"

But man says: "I am too busy now; I have work to do. I can't take time to look for You." And the Lord says: "I will wait."—*Paramahansa Yogananda, "Sayings of Yogananda"*

We put forth our hands to receive God's gifts of life and sun and food and all the other things He bestows on us; but even as we receive them, we are unmindful of the Giver. If you have lovingly given presents to someone and then find out that he never thinks of you, how hurt you would feel! God feels that way, too.—*Paramahansa Yogananda, "Man's Eternal Quest"*

India, in the person of one of her great masters, Paramahansa Yogananda, has brought to us this priceless knowledge of soul-realization. How grateful we should be to a people whose greatest men, down the centuries, have given their lives, have renounced everything else, in order to explore the divine potentialities in man! What India has given us today in Paramahansaji's teachings is worth more to us than anything we could give to India in exchange. Today the Western man is in dire need of a spiritual technique for developing his soul resources. That technique is *Kriya Yoga,* an ancient science brought to us for the first time by a master from India.—*Rajarsi Janakananda, "Rajarsi Janakananda: Great Western Yogi"*

Nothing in the world is as divinely intoxicating as my beloved God. I drink unceasingly of that Nectar. "O aged Wine of my Soul, as I drink of Thee from the ocean within me, I find Thou art inexhaustible. Thou art a skyful of happiness that displays all the stars of the universe, ever throbbing within my heart."—*Paramahansa Yogananda, "Thanksgiving Message"*

Always in the background of your mind hum a silent devotional song of love to your beloved Heavenly Father, remembering that all your abilities are gifts from Him.—*Paramahansa Yogananda, SRF Lessons*

O Father, when I was blind I found not a door that led to Thee. Thou hast healed my eyes; now I discover doors everywhere: the hearts of flowers, the voices of friendship, memories of lovely experiences. Each gust of my prayer opens a new entrance to the vast temple of Thy presence.—*Paramahansa Yogananda, "Whispers from Eternity"*

SPECIAL THOUGHT FOR DECEMBER

The real celebration of Christmas is the realization within ourselves of Christ Consciousness. It is of utmost importance to every man, whatever his religion, that he experience within himself this "birth" of the universal Christ.

The universe is the body of Christ: everywhere present within it, without limitation, is the Christ Consciousness. When you can close your eyes and by meditation expand your awareness until you feel the whole universe as your own body, Christ will have been born within you. You will know that your mind is a little wave of that ocean of Cosmic Consciousness in which Christ dwells.

Self-Realization Fellowship has started the idea of devoting one day at Christmastime entirely to meditative worship of Christ, and that idea shall never die. Just as we at the Los Angeles headquarters celebrate the birthday of Jesus spiritually by an all-day meditation on December 23rd, let the 23rd be used by all devotees of Christ for the spiritual Christmas; pass the entire day in ever-increasingly deep meditation. Then spend December 25th as the social Christmas, observing the festivities of the sacred season with relatives and friends.

One of the most encouraging signs of a spiritual rebirth in the world today is the increased willingness of Christians to observe the birth of Jesus by these long meditation meetings. This spiritual custom of Christmas meditation will in time be adopted by all Christians—I predict it.—*Paramahansa Yogananda, "Self-Realization Magazine"*

The spiritual path is like a razor's edge. It is not simple at all. Seclusion is the price of greatness and God-realization. When I am alone I am with God. That is the way you should be.—*Paramahansa Yogananda, in a talk to disciples*

Don't mix with others too closely. Friendships do not satisfy us unless they are rooted in mutual love for the Lord. Our human wish for loving understanding from others is in reality the soul's desire for unity with God. The more we seek to satisfy that desire outwardly, the less likely we are to find the Divine Companion.—*Paramahansa Yogananda, "Sayings of Yogananda"*

Keep a diary of your spiritual life. I used to make a record of how long I had meditated daily and how deep I had gone. Seek solitude as much as possible. Do not spend your leisure time with other people for merely social purposes. God's love is hard to find in company.—*Paramahansa Yogananda, "Self-Realization Magazine"*

"I am going to the hills to be alone with God," a student informed Paramahansa Yogananda.

"You will not advance spiritually in that way," Paramahansaji replied. "Your mind is not yet ready to concentrate deeply on Spirit. Your thoughts will dwell mostly on memories of people and worldly pastimes, even though you remain in a cave. Cheerful performance of your earthly duties, coupled with daily meditation, is the better path."—*Paramahansa Yogananda, "Sayings of Yogananda"*

So long as you have not found God, it is best not to be interested in amusements. Seeking diversion means forgetting Him. First learn to love Him and know Him. Then it won't matter what you do, for He will never leave your thoughts.—*Paramahansa Yogananda, "Sayings of Yogananda"*

Don't joke all the time with each other. Be happy and cheerful inside. Why dissipate in useless talk the perceptions you have gained? Words are like bullets: when you spend their force in idle conversation, your supply of inner ammunition is wasted. Your consciousness is like a milk pail: when you fill it with the peace of meditation you ought to keep it that way. Joking is often false fun that drives holes in the sides of your bucket and allows all the milk of your peace to run out.—*Paramahansa Yogananda, in a talk to disciples*

Be alone within. Don't lead the aimless life that so many persons follow. Meditate and read good books more....Once in a while it is all right to go to the movies and have a little social life, but mostly remain apart and live within yourself....Enjoy solitude; but when you want to mix with others, do so with all your love and friendship, so that those persons cannot forget you, but remember always that they met someone who inspired them and turned their minds toward God.—*Paramahansa Yogananda, "Man's Eternal Quest"*

The true practice of religion is to sit still in meditation and talk to God. But you don't get to that point of intensity, you don't concentrate enough, and that is why you remain in delusion.—*Paramahansa Yogananda, "Man's Eternal Quest"*

The silence habitual to Sri Yukteswar was caused by his deep perceptions of the Infinite. No time remained for the interminable "revelations" that occupy the days of teachers without Self-realization. A saying from the Hindu scriptures is: "In shallow men the fish of little thoughts cause much commotion. In oceanic minds the whales of inspiration make hardly a ruffle."—*Paramahansa Yogananda, "Autobiography of a Yogi"*

Be with people in silence; don't spend precious time and energy in idle talk. Eat in silence; work in silence. God loves silence.—*Paramahansa Yogananda, SRF Lessons*

Build your inner environment. Practice silence! I remember the wonderful discipline of the Great Ones. When we used to talk and chatter, they would say: "Go back into your inner castle." It was very hard to comprehend then, but now I understand the way of peace that we were shown.—*Paramahansa Yogananda, SRF Lessons*

My Silence, like an expanding sphere, spreads everywhere.

My silence spreads like a radio song, above, beneath, left and right, within and without.

My silence spreads like a wildfire of bliss; the dark thickets of sorrow and tall oaks of pride are all burning up.

My silence, like the ether, passes through everything, carrying the songs of earth, atoms, and stars into the halls of His infinite mansion.—*Paramahansa Yogananda, "Metaphysical Meditations"*

You should sit in silence before deciding about any important matter, asking the Father for His blessing. Then behind your power is God's power; behind your mind His mind; behind your will His will.—*Paramahansa Yogananda, "The Law of Success"*

From the depths of silence the geyser of God's bliss shoots up unfailingly and flows over man's being.— *Paramahansa Yogananda, "Sayings of Yogananda"*

To bring divine awareness into our human consciousness we must outgrow the limited conventional concept of Christ. To me Christmas is a thought of spiritual grandeur—a realization that our minds are an altar of Christ, the Universal Intelligence in all creation. Jesus was born in a little crib, but the Christ Spirit is omnipresent.—*Paramahansa Yogananda, "Self-Realization Magazine"*

I will prepare for the coming of the Omnipresent Baby Christ by cleaning the cradle of my consciousness, now rusty with selfishness, indifference, and sense attachments; and by polishing it with deep, daily, divine meditation, introspection, and discrimination. I will remodel the cradle with the dazzling soul-qualities of brotherly love, humbleness, faith, desire for God-realization, will power, self-control, renunciation, and unselfishness, that I may fittingly celebrate the birth of the Divine Child.— *Paramahansa Yogananda, "Metaphysical Meditations"*

Christ is born in the cradle of tenderness. Love is a greater power than hate. Whatever you say, say it with love. Harm no one. Judge not others. Hate none, love all; behold Christ in all. Think of everything in terms of universality.—*Paramahansa Yogananda, "Self-Realization Magazine"*

Lift your eyes and concentrate within. Behold the astral star of divine wisdom and let the wise thoughts in you follow that telescopic star to behold the Christ everywhere.

In that land of everlasting Christmas, of festive, omnipresent Christ Consciousness, you will find Jesus, Krishna, the saints of all religions, the great guru-preceptors waiting to give you a divine floral reception of everlasting happiness.—*Paramahansa Yogananda, "Metaphysical Meditations"*

Will Jesus come again? Metaphysically, he is already omnipresent. He smiles at you through every flower. He feels his cosmic body in every speck of space. Every movement of the wind breathes the breath of Jesus. Through his oneness with the divine Christ Consciousness he is incarnate in all that lives. If you have eyes to behold, you can see him enthroned throughout creation.—*Paramahansa Yogananda, "Man's Eternal Quest"*

There is a vast difference between imagination and Self-realization. Through your imagination you may have subconscious dreams and visions of Christ every day. But such experiences do not mean that you are truly in touch with him. The real visitation of Jesus is the communion with Christ Consciousness. If you are in tune with that Christ, your whole life will change.—*Paramahansa Yogananda, "Self-Realization Magazine"*

O Christ, take possession of my heart and mind! Be thou reborn in me as love for all men. May thy consciousness which is in every atom manifest in me as unconditional loyalty to Guru and the Great Ones, and to thee, O Blessed Jesus, and to the Supreme who is the Father of all.—*Paramahansa Yogananda, "Self-Realization Magazine"*

Coax Christ today with your songs and the devotion of your heart, and then coax him with your deepening Self-realization. With all the intensity of your zeal and inner perception, merge your consciousness in the happiness within. Forget time. When you feel joy spreading within you, realize that Christ is hearing your song. You are not identified with Christ if your concentration is merely on the words. But if your joy is singing within, Christ is listening to you.—*Paramahansa Yogananda, "Self-Realization Magazine"*

Through the transparency of my deepest meditation I will receive the light of the Father passing through
me. I will be a son of God, even as Jesus was, by receiv-
ing God fully through my meditation-expanded soul
consciousness. I will follow the shepherds of faith,
devotion, and meditation, who will lead me through
the star of inner wisdom to the omnipresent Christ.
—*Paramahansa Yogananda, "Self-Realization Magazine"*

All my thoughts are decorating the Christmas tree of meditation with the rare gifts of devotion, sealed with golden heart-prayers that Christ may come and receive my humble gifts.

I will mentally join in the worship in all mosques, churches, and temples; and perceive the birth of the universal Christ Consciousness as peace on the altar of all devotional hearts.—*Paramahansa Yogananda, "Metaphysical Meditations"*

May the Christmas spirit you feel not end with today; rather may it be with you every night as you meditate. Then in the silence of your own mind, as you drive away all restless thoughts, Christ Consciousness will come. If we all follow the spirit of Jesus we shall surely experience every day his presence within us.—*Paramahansa Yogananda, "Man's Eternal Quest"*

And so, dear ones, my Christmas will go on forever, in ever increasing joy everlasting. If this joy were limited, as worldly happiness is, a time would come when all would be finished. But no saint will ever be able to exhaust the ever-new bliss of God.
—*Paramahansa Yogananda, "Man's Eternal Quest"*

When tilling ground for the cultivation of crops, one needs patience to destroy all useless weeds; and to wait, even though the ground then appears barren, until the hidden good seeds sprout into plants. It requires still more patience to clear the field of consciousness that is overgrown with weeds of useless attachments to sense pleasures, which are very difficult to uproot. Yet when the field of consciousness is cleared, and sown with seeds of good qualities, plants of noble activities sprout forth, yielding abundantly the fruits of real happiness. Above all, have patience to seek communion with God through deep meditation and to become acquainted with your indestructible soul, hidden within your perishable earthly body.—*Paramahansa Yogananda, in a "Para-gram"*

The truth is: that which you want is with you all the time, closer than hands or feet. Any moment it may lift you above the world and personal depression. Wait patiently for Him.—*Sister Gyanamata, "Self-Realization Magazine"*

Do not look for a spiritual flower every day. Sow the seed, water it with prayer and right endeavor. When it sprouts, take care of the plant, pulling out the weeds of doubt, indecision, and indifference that may spring up around it. Some morning you will suddenly behold your long-awaited spiritual flower of Realization.—*Paramahansa Yogananda, in a "Para-gram"*

You are your own enemy and you don't know it.
You don't learn to sit quietly. You don't learn to give
time to God. And you are impatient and expect to attain heaven all at once. You cannot get it by reading
books or by listening to sermons or by doing chari-
table works. You can get it only by giving your time
to Him in deep meditation.—*Paramahansa Yogananda*,
"Man's Eternal Quest"

Let us forget the sorrows of the past and make up our minds not to dwell on them in the New Year. With determination and unflinching will, let us renew our lives, our good habits, and our successes. If the last year has been hopelessly bad, the New Year must be hopefully good.—*Paramahansa Yogananda, "Self-Realization Magazine"*